The Pursuit of Liberty

The
Pursuit
of
Liberty

Can the Ideals That Made America Great Provide a Model for the World?

edited by James Piereson

A Collection of Essays from
The American Spectator

Encounter Books New York · London

First edition published in 2008 by Encounter Books,
an activity of Encounter for Culture and Education, Inc.,
a nonprofit, tax exempt corporation.
Encounter Books website address: www.encounterbooks.com

Manufactured in the United States and printed on
acid-free paper. The paper used in this publication meets
the minimum requirements of ANSI/NISO Z39.48–1992
(R 1997) (*Permanence of Paper*).

FIRST EDITION
Essays from this collection first appeared in *The American Spectator*.

LIBRARY OF CONGRESS CATALOGING-IN-PUBLICATION DATA

The pursuit of liberty: can the ideals that made America great
provide a model for the world?/James Piereson, ed.
p. cm.
Includes index.
ISBN-13: 978-1-59403-238-7 (hardcover : alk. paper)
ISBN-10: 1-59403-238-6 (hardcover: alk. paper) 1. Liberty. 2. Democracy.
3. World politics—21st century. I. Piereson, James.
JC585.P87 2009
320.01'1—dc22
2008053918

10 9 8 7 6 5 4 3 2 1

Contents

Preface

On the day that he left office in 1809, Thomas Jefferson observed to the citizens of Washington, D.C. that, "The station which we occupy among the nations of the earth is honorable, but awful. Trusted with the destinies of this solitary republic of the world, the only monument of human rights, and the sole depository of the sacred fire of freedom and self-government, from hence it is to be lighted up in other regions of the earth, if other regions of the earth shall ever become susceptible of its benign influence." Jefferson thus sounded a theme (and perhaps even inaugurated it) that would echo through the generations in American debates over foreign policy, and one that was to be carried forward by some of his most prominent successors, including most especially Presidents Lincoln, Wilson, Roosevelt (Franklin), Kennedy, and Reagan.

Americans have long viewed their democratic institutions as models for adoption by the rest of the world; and they have long believed that the security of their own experiment in popular government was bound up with the spread of liberty elsewhere to peoples still ground down by tyranny or despotism.

Jefferson, of course, spoke in an era when the American republic could still be described as a novel experiment and when its survival was very much in doubt within an international system controlled by states possessed of far greater military and commercial power. Jefferson and his compatriots understood very well that some of these states would like nothing better than to strangle the infant republic in its crib. They thus looked to the outside world from a dual perspective, at times fearing it and at others wishing to reform it. The United States was a weak nation, a lamb surrounded by wolves, but also one armed with a powerful idea that might in time turn the affairs of nations in a favorable direction.

The rise of the United States as an international power during the twentieth century did not diminish for Americans the appeal of Jefferson's vision, but it did alter greatly the circumstances to which it was applied. As a world power in its own right, it was no longer at the mercy of stronger adversaries; indeed, the United States now had the military and commercial strength to project that vision around the globe. The wary eye with which Jefferson looked out toward England and France was increasingly turned back on the United States by the outside world now suspicious of its overwhelming power. Americans, too, always ambivalent about the exercise of power, wondered how far their country should go, and in what ways it was legitimate, to export its ideals and institutions elsewhere.

These broad and enduring issues were joined once again in American history in the aftermath of the terrorist attacks of September 11, 2001 and the subsequent invasions of Afghanistan and Iraq. President Bush, sounding a Jeffersonian theme, declared in his 2005 Inaugural Address that, "We are led by events and by common sense to one conclusion: the best hope of liberty in our land increasingly depends on the success of liberty in other lands. The best hope for peace in our world is the expansion of freedom in the world." The President thus linked an idealistic campaign to promote freedom with the nation's interests in peace and security.

The difficulty of the war in Iraq, however, and the failure of coalition troops to locate the weapons of mass destruction that supplied one of the justifications for the invasion, has ignited a now long-running debate on America's role in the contemporary world and the degree to which it is legitimate or even in its interests to deploy military force to install democratic institutions in foreign lands. This debate is of crucial importance because, just as the conclusions drawn from the disputes over the Vietnam conflict cast a shadow over future policy, so will the outcome of our current debates influence American policy for decades to come.

Can the ideals that made America great serve as a model for the rest of the world? To what degree should American foreign policy be crafted with an eye to promoting democracy and freedom abroad? In a creedal nation like the United States, can we usefully distinguish between its ideals and its interests? How will the outcome of the Iraq conflict influence the nation's capacity to promote its ideals in the future? Was President Bush correct to say that the most effective means of defeating Islamic radicalism is by confronting it with our ideals of democracy and liberty?

These (and other) questions were posed to an eminent group of expert authors who composed their answers in a series of ten essays that were published on a near-monthly basis in *The American Spectator* beginning in September 2006 and concluding in September 2007. The writers invited to participate in the series make up an impressive list: James Q. Wilson, James Kurth, Norman Podhoretz, Lawrence Harrison, Daniel Johnson, Fouad Ajami, Michael Novak, Natan Sharansky and Rod Dermer, Victor Davis Hanson, and Andrew Roberts. While most on this list are conservative or at least moderate in their general outlooks, they have taken different positions on the war in Iraq, the stakes at issue in that conflict, and the degree to which the promotion of democracy should be deployed as an instrument of U.S. foreign policy. These disparate points of view will be apparent to readers of the essays now collected in this volume. It should also be noted that several authors—Johnson, Ajami, Sharansky and Dermer, and Roberts—bring European or Middle Eastern perspectives to the discussion.

These essays were compiled from mid-2006 to mid-2007 at precisely the point at which the conflict in Iraq reached its most difficult juncture and when President Bush responded to that crisis with a "surge" of new troops which signaled a re-dedication to winning the battle in that country against foreign terrorists and domestic insurgents. Thus, though the authors were not able to incorporate the promising trajectory of the surge into their reflections, they were able to take into account the intensifying domestic debate over the war that led to Democratic gains in the 2006 congressional elections. The authors were thus in a position to understand the difficulties of the war that stood in the way of any immediate resolution of it and to respond to the developing arguments in opposition to it which seemed to be gaining favor among the voters.

At the same time, these essays reach beyond the immediate war in Iraq and the conflict against Islamism to consider larger questions of how these conflicts fit into the tradition of U.S. foreign policy, America's role in the world in the twenty-first century, and the prospects for using military force either to promote democracy or, even, to defend important national interests. The purpose of these essays is partly to inform the present debate but also to enlarge it by bringing into play these broader issues that are bound to arise again in future conflicts.

In collecting and preparing these essays for publication, the editor is grateful to Alfred S. Regnery, the publisher of *The American Spectator* and a distinguished author and editor in his own right, for his sage advice and assistance in recommending authors and selecting topics for the series. Roger Kimball, the publisher of Encounter books and the editor of *The New Criterion*, contributed his broad knowledge and editorial insight (along with his friendship) in ways too numerous to acknowledge. The project could not have been completed without their sustained assistance. Of course, the editor is also grateful to the distinguished authors for their contributions to the volume.

The John Templeton Foundation generously provided financial support for both the essay series in *The American Spectator* and the publication of the edited volume. While the participants in the project are grateful for the Foundation's support, it should go without saying that the opinions expressed in these essays are those of the authors alone and do not necessarily reflect the views of the trustees and staff of the John Templeton Foundation.

—James Piereson

American Exceptionalism

James Q. Wilson

Professor Wilson reminds us of the caution with which the U.S. must proceed in its admirable efforts to advance the cause of liberty and freedom in the world. Because American institutions are unique and adapted to our own history, we cannot expect other nations to imitate our practices when they embark on their own experiments in democratic government. Unfortunately, much of what the rest of the world knows about America is transmitted through our movies, television, music, and other instruments of our popular culture. America's influence abroad would be more constructive, he suggests, if we promoted a different portrait of our country that emphasized our love of freedom, our respect for talent and achievement, and our willingness to forego imperial ambitions even when we have the power to pursue them.

WHEN PRESIDENT BUSH said that America hopes to spread democracy to the entire world, he was echoing a sentiment many people support. Though Americans do not put "extending democracy" near the top of their list of foreign policy objectives (preventing terrorism is their chief goal), few would deny that if popular rule is extended it would improve lives around the world.

Democracy, of course, means rule by the people. But the devil is in the details. By one count, the number of democracies quintupled in the second half of the twentieth century, but there are freedom-loving and freedom-disdaining democracies. Fareed Zakaria calls the latter "illiberal democracies." Among them are Kazakhstan, Pakistan, Ukraine, and Venezuela.

The number of democratic regimes has grown rapidly in the last several decades, but what has grown is not like American-style democracy. Though most democracies have certain things in common—popular elections, the rule of law, and rights for minorities—we should never suppose that what we hope will appear in the Middle East and elsewhere will look like American government any more than Britain, France, Germany, India, Japan, or Turkey look like us. Recall that American democracy contains some strikingly undemocratic features, such as an Electoral College, two senators for each state regardless of state populations, and an independent judiciary.

America differs from other democratic nations in many ways, some material and some mental. It has a more rapidly growing economy than most of Europe and deeper sense of patriotism than almost any other country with popular rule. A recent survey of 91,000 people in fifty nations, conducted by the Pew Research Center and reported on by Andrew Kohut and Bruce Stokes, outlines our political culture and shows how different it is from those in most other democracies.

Americans identify more strongly with their own country than do people in many affluent democracies. While 71 percent of Americans say they are "very proud" to be in America, only 38 percent of the French and 21 percent of the Germans and the Japanese say they are proud to live in their countries. And Americans are much more committed to individualism than are people elsewhere. Only one-third of Americans, but two-thirds of Germans and Italians, think that success in life is determined by forces outside their own control. This message is one that Americans wish to transmit to their children: 60 percent say that children should be taught the value of hard work, but only one-third of the British and Italians and one-fifth of the Germans agree. Over half of all Americans think that economic competition is good because it stimulates people to work hard and develop new ideas; only one-third of French and Spanish people agree. Americans would like their views to spread throughout the world: over three-fourths said this was a good idea, compared to only one-fourth of the people in France, Germany, and Italy and one-third of those in Great Britain.

In 1835 Alexis de Tocqueville discussed American exception-alism in *Democracy in America*, and he is still correct. There was then and there continues now to be in this country a remarkable com-mitment to liberty, egalitarianism, individualism, and laissez-faire values. He gave three explanations for this state of affairs: We came to occupy a vast, largely empty, and isolated continent; we have ben-efited from a legal system that involves federalism and an indepen-dent judiciary; and we have embraced certain "habits of the heart" that were profoundly shaped by our religious tradition. Of these, Tocqueville rightly said that our customs were more important than our laws and our laws more important than our geography. What is remarkable today is that a vast nation of around 300 million people still shares views once held by a few million crowded along the Eastern seaboard.

THE CONSTITUTION

Our constitutional system is, I think, even more important than it was to Tocqueville's mind. He wrote about federalism, local town-ship government, and an independent judiciary but neglected the system of separated powers and the checks and balances each branch imposes on the other two. Federalism, he correctly under-stood, keeps government close to the people, but the separate branches of the national government, each of which shares power with the others, impede the rate of change in ways that make it both difficult to adopt new policies and hard to change old ones.

America was slow to adopt welfare programs, social security, unemployment insurance, and government-supported health care, while Europe adopted these policies rapidly. We have kept our tax rate lower than it is in most of Europe. The central difference is not that Europeans are either smarter or dumber than we, but that a parliamentary system permits temporary popular majorities to make bold changes rather quickly, whereas a presidential system with a powerful, independent, and internally divided Congress requires that big changes undergo lengthy debates and substantive accommodations. On occasion America does act like a parliamentary system, as it did under Franklin Roosevelt during the Great Depression and under Lyndon Johnson when he commanded extraordinary majorities in both houses of Congress.

The system a country uses to elect its rulers also makes a difference. In a recent study, political scientists Torben Iversen and David Soskice have shown that, among seventeen large democracies, those that elect their legislators using proportional representation (PR) are three times more likely than those electing them by majority vote to have leftist governments that redistribute income from rich to poor.

Australia, Canada, Japan, Great Britain, and the United States (among others) have majoritarian systems, while Austria, Germany, Italy, and Sweden (among others) have PR systems. Under a PR system, several parties will compete, while in majoritarian systems, only two parties usually contest elections. If there are several parties, middle-class voters will support programs that tax the rich and benefit them, knowing that they can change their voting habits if a government wishes to tax them more. But if there are only two major parties, middle-class voters will worry that voting for leftist parties will mean more taxes for them, and so they will be inclined to support right-wing parties.

4

As we struggle to rescue Medicare and Social Security from their inevitable bankruptcy, we are learning that correcting old programs is as difficult as inventing them in the first place. How well our constitutional system will handle these problems remains to be seen, but some changes will surely occur: the government cannot abandon programs that are as popular as these. Already national commissions have reported on both, though so far with little effect.

Our constitutional system is, of course, no guarantee against making mistakes. When President John Adams was in office, Congress passed the Alien and Sedition Acts; after we entered the First World War we experienced an overblown Red Scare; it took a century after the Civil War before Congress was willing to pass laws ending racial discrimination; and of late the Bipartisan Campaign Reform Act, written by Senators John McCain and Russell Feingold, constitutes a massive attack on the First Amendment rights of various interest groups.

But parliamentary systems do no better. England gave us homegrown fascism in the person of Oswald Mosley; France expressed its anti-Semitism in the Dreyfus Affair; and today much of Europe is in the grip of deep tensions between Muslims whom it will not assimilate and native Europeans who want Muslim labor but not Muslim rights. America, by contrast, has managed to absorb every immigrant group in ways that enrich the country and convert most new arrivals into patriots. We have several million Muslims living here, but I suspect that the proportion who embrace the radical fascism of Muslim extremists is smaller here than abroad.

FEDERALISM

Federalism keeps government close to the people, especially with respect to issues that mean a lot to them. The police, the schools, criminal justice, and land-use planning are deeply local matters. As a result, we have more variation in the policies of these agencies than one would find in a centralized democracy. As school quality becomes a problem, some states allow the creation of charter schools and a few places accept voucher programs. Land use planning can be either greatly restrictive or open to new developments, depending on the policies of cities and counties.

Federalism, of course, has costs as well as benefits. Southern states practiced racial discrimination after most northern ones had passed laws against it. Locally elected school boards can often be captured by the electoral power of teachers' unions, thus creating a dubious bargaining arrangement: School boards that are supposed to negotiate with teachers over salaries and working conditions often are the captive of the very teachers with whom they must do business.

But the benefits are just as clear. When welfare reform began at the national level, it built on new ideas being tried in several states. When limits on aggressive medical malpractice suits began, they came first in states and are only now being considered in Washington. These changes confirm the argument by Justice Louis Brandeis that federalism is valuable because it creates "laboratories of democracy." He was explaining why much good comes from political alternatives. Not only can government choose what to do, people can choose among states where it is done. People who want medical marijuana, tough environmental laws, lenient criminal justice penalties, and alternative lifestyles can live in one place; people who prefer the opposites of these can live elsewhere.

By keeping certain policies close to the people, government here cannot long ignore popular demands. Consider crime. When our crime rates began to rise in the early 1960s, Barry Goldwater, the Republican presidential candidate in 1964, campaigned about "crime in the streets." Many of his opponents berated him, claiming, wrongly, that his concern was a mask for a hostility to racial minorities. But Lyndon Johnson, who defeated Goldwater, knew better. Since people were worried about crime, he created a national commission on crime and the administration of justice that issued a multi-volume report.

But far more important than a national commission is the fact that every district attorney, every mayor, every governor, and many judges are elected by the people. When crime became a public concern, these officials had to respond. By the early 1980s, that response had led to a higher proportion of convicted criminals going to prison where they served longer sentences. In Europe, by contrast, crime rates also rose but this fact was confronted by political elites who were insulated from public concern.

The difference can be seen in the contrast between America and England. In the 1970s, England had lower robbery and burglary rates than did California, probably because the former sent a higher proportion of robbers to prison than did the latter. But by the mid-1980s, the criminal justice policies of the two countries had switched places. America, driven by popular pressure, increased the proportion of convicted offenders sent to prison while England reduced that proportion. Crime rates fell in America and rose in England. By the early 1990s, England had a robbery rate higher than America's and a burglary rate that was twice as high as ours. We cannot be certain that differing punishment policies explain the changes in crime rates, but no other plausible explanation is available.

During many of these changes, Ronald Reagan was president of the United States and Margaret Thatcher the prime minister of England. I doubt they disagreed about crime or how to deal with it. What is important is not that they were in office but that in this country scores of elected prosecutors endorsed popular new policies while in England scores of appointed prosecutors did not.

When public officials are appointed, they acquire a certain detachment from public opinion, thereby enabling them to act on the basis of their personal beliefs. Those beliefs, in my experience, consist of some combination of self-interest and a therapeutic ideology. The self-interest of British civil servants has been memorably recorded in *Yes, Minister* and *Yes, Prime Minister*, two BBC television series that I believe are not only hilarious but accurate. It would be almost impossible to make such a program about American civil servants, not because they care less for their own advantage but because they are checked by competing elected officials in legislative committees who are highly sensitive to what the public wants.

These differences are dramatized by differing American and English policies toward the death penalty. In both countries a majority of the people support it, but only in America does it exist. And it exists in most states but not all. In England, parliamentary leaders do not propose the idea for enactment even though people want it.

As with the choices offered by federalism, so also with its easy transmission of public opinion: the right decision is not always made. In some states, the public can back unconstitutional or morally dubious arguments. The courts will ordinarily prevent the former from taking effect, but nothing will prevent the latter. But human choice makes a difference: If a state makes a series of popular but questionable choices, people can move to a different state. Moreover, the states must compete with one another for business. A firm wishing to build a factory or an office building will examine not only land costs but tax rates and political attitudes, picking the state that offers the best deal. This competition imposes a powerful brake on ill-considered schemes.

RELIGION

Tocqueville ascribed our political culture in large part to our religious heritage. Our settlers who escaped religious persecution at home brought with them a form of Christian worship that was both "democratic and republican." To be sure, some Americans in 1835 and many more today "profess Christian dogma . . . because they are afraid of not looking like they believe them." But for most people, religion is a reality, not a dodge. Tocqueville understood that, contrary to the prediction of European philosophers, freedom and enlightenment would not extinguish religious zeal. On the contrary: here freedom largely explains our persistent religiosity.

That is because a nation that never had an established church and did not grant money or privileges to existing churches left religion in the hands of spiritual entrepreneurs. These people were sometimes domestic missionaries and sometimes local citizens eager to create and govern a religious organization. Protestant churches had to compete in a spiritual marketplace, with many new churches emerging every year, people changing their affiliations frequently, and a few mega-churches emerging under the guidance of the most successful ministers. The system of natural liberty that Adam Smith said would benefit the economy has also aided religion.

As a result, nearly half of all Americans attend churches or synagogues weekly compared to 4 percent of the English, 5 percent of the French, and comparably low levels in most of Western Europe. Some may suspect that our religiosity is sustained by recent immigrants, especially those from Latin America. But that is only part of the story. Churches grew in membership between 1776 and 1850, long before Irish and Italian immigrants arrived in any number. When German immigrants arrived toward the end of the nineteenth century, they behaved like Germans still in their homeland: most were nonobservant Lutherans. But by the time they had become third-generation Americans, they acquired the church commitments of America generally and went to church frequently. And the Mormon church has grown rapidly without, at least in America, emphasizing immigrant recruitment.

In most of Europe, by contrast, religion was allied with politics so that over the centuries European secularists, as one scholar has noted, "hounded Christians as political enemies rather than as religious adversaries." As a result, European churches that are still under government influence in much of Europe long after these nations had become secular create a political failure. As Tocqueville put it, "religion increases its power over some and loses the hope of reigning over all."

Religion in America has helped train citizens on self-government by giving them independent congregations to manage even in places that when first settled had no civil government. The struggle between religious faiths has at times been acute, as with Protestant attacks on the Roman Catholic Church in the nineteenth and early twentieth centuries. But this rivalry was suppressed by the courts, weakened by the slow realization that Catholics here were Americans first and Catholics second, and by the election of a Catholic president in 1960. As with the economy, so with religion: markets generate mutual understanding far better than monopolies.

Religion has powerfully affected American politics: Its leaders were at the forefront of efforts to abolish slavery and still struggle over war, abortion, and gay rights. Indeed, among white voters in the 2004 presidential election, religious differences explained a larger fraction of their votes than did their age, sex, income, or education. At the extremes, religion can lead to violence, as when some radical fundamentalists bombed abortion clinics or radical secularists sustained the Weather Underground. But for most people, religion has a moderate impact despite the fervent rhetoric directed at it by several contributors to the *New York Times*.

Religion in America explains a host of worthwhile traits. As Arthur Brooks shows in the new book, *Who Really Cares*, people who are religious are more likely to live in two-parent families, achieve upward economic mobility, resist the lures of drugs and crime, and overcome health problems. Religious people are more likely to give to charity, including secular ones, than are non-religious people, and they are more likely to donate blood, give food or money to homeless persons, and to return excessive change mistakenly given to them by a cashier.

Religion, of course, cannot be the sole guide to a useful democracy. People who believe that their faith justifies their desire to dominate other people or to destroy the infidels are on a crash course toward social destruction. Iran is an example. And a country in which a secular autocrat has imposed draconian rule as a way of curbing the excesses of religion has created an alternative no better than the one he suppressed. Iraq under Saddam Hussein is an example.

Religion requires constitutional boundaries to limit the radical demands of a few. But constitutional government without religion may, as the examples cited earlier in this suggest, give to people no sense of common destiny nor any faith in the transcendent value of their principles.

FREEDOM

No matter how many mistakes they make in understanding the Bill of Rights, no matter how many times they may support policies hostile to liberty, Americans share at a deep level a commitment to freedom. Ask almost any member of the Armed Forces why they are fighting in Afghanistan or Iraq, the most common answer is that they are "defending freedom." Ask almost any citizen what it is they like most about this country, and they will say its freedom.

Now, fighting in the Middle East involves a lot of issues that have little to do with freedom in America and many American domestic polices often reduce freedom. But despite that, our verbal commitment to this goal is real. And this view means that Americans tend to define the issues that divide them as a contest of rights more than as a matter of choice.

We see this in the flood of lawsuits by which Americans tend to manage their differences. Some people think that this is because we have too many lawyers, and a few have suggested that to solve the problem we close our law schools for five years. And it is true that we have, in proportion to our population, three times as many lawyers as does Great Britain and twenty-five times as many as Japan.

But we are not more litigious because we have more lawyers; we have more lawyers because we are so litigious. Not even the framers of the Constitution anticipated this. As Alexander Hamilton put it in *Federalist* Number 78, "the judiciary . . . has no influence over either the sword or the purse, no direction of either the strength or the wealth of the society, and can take no active resolution whatever." As a result, "the judiciary is beyond comparison the weakest of the three departments of power." Things turned out a bit differently than Hamilton supposed. The courts have become immensely powerful for two reasons: the existence of an independent judiciary and the beliefs Americans have about the foundation of their government.

Courts that are independent of the legislative and executive branches will inevitably become the referee that determines when a law or order violates the Constitution. That document did not say this, but it did say that it was the supreme law of the land. That being so, there must be some organization that will defend that claim. Early on, the Supreme Court under the leadership of John Marshall became that entity, and since then no one has doubted it. As the federal government grew in size and authority, more and more issues arose that implicated the Constitution, and so more and more often the Court decided how that document should be read. Since 1789, the Supreme Court has declared more than 160 laws to be unconstitutional.

But far more important than judicial review in explaining America's commitment to rights has been the legacy of the Revolutionary War and the sentiments expressed in the Declaration of Independence. That document said that "all men are created equal" and are "endowed by their Creator with certain unalienable rights" that include "life, liberty, and the pursuit of happiness." To secure these rights, governments are created that derive their "just powers from the consent of the governed."

This language has had a lasting influence over how Americans think about government even though the Supreme Court has rarely made any reference to the Declaration and lawyers are not trained to think that this document has any legal value. To judges and attorneys, the Declaration has no more authority, and probably less, than does the preamble to the Constitution. But to Americans, the language of the Declaration is remembered far more clearly than that of the Constitution. Even though in 1776 neither women nor slaves could vote, we recall the claim that we were created equal. Though the government may imprison or execute criminals and send soldiers off to die, we have a right to life, liberty, and the pursuit of happiness (though not to happiness itself).

This language fits well with the fact that in America we had no direct experience with a hereditary aristocracy or with a king who could rule by divine right. As the country expanded west beyond the few million along the Atlantic coast, Americans took with them a shared view of equality with its accompanying hostility to displays of superiority and a desire for each person to be esteemed and have a fair share in government. They also embraced a desire for liberty, but not license; that is, the freedom to act in accord with decent principles, many of them religiously defined. As towns were organized, these principles shaped their governance, not because Thomas Jefferson had written them but because Americans shared these views before they tried to design any local political arrangements.

This tradition has equipped Americans with a commitment to natural law: that is, to a belief that laws cannot be justified simply as the commands of a ruler but only as an expression of some higher standard that endows people with claims against both other people and the government itself if either oversteps what we believe to be the right standards of conduct. This commitment helps us understand an otherwise puzzling fact: Americans typically have a low opinion of our governing institutions, especially Congress, but an exceptionally high opinion of the constitutional system of which they are a part.

These views impose constraints on what government might do. In Europe, the slow replacement of kings with elected parliaments did not alter the general assumption that the people owed the government something, namely, a respect for authority. In America, as Seymour Martin Lipset has argued, people who had that view (the Loyalists) emigrated to Canada while those who thought the government owed respect to the people remained and fought as revolutionaries. The differences in outlook persist to this day. Canada has a larger welfare state than the United States in part because Canadians (notably those in the east) want welfare and Americans (notably those in the middle and far west) do not.

The consequence of these views is that Americans today practice adversarial politics, not deferential ones, and turn frequently to the courts to settle their differences in a struggle over rights. Every government agency here operates under close public scrutiny by the press, interest groups, and on occasion an aroused public. We see the result in environmental policies. In England and Sweden, these policies tend to be made by a collaborative and often unpublicized accord among business firms, labor unions, environmental groups, and government agencies. Here, by contrast, they are made in a hotly contested public struggle that pits firms, unions, groups, and agencies against one another.

SPREADING DEMOCRACY

There are many different kinds of democracy that can be spread, and Americans should never suppose that what may take hold in another country will closely resemble what has grown up here. A few may be illiberal ones, many will be elitist ones, but most will enhance the freedom of their people, change governments peacefully after an election is held, and refrain from the use of force to conquer other nations.

Some Americans are skeptical that democracy can be exported, especially to the Middle East. These countries lack what we had: a successful war against a colonial power, wise statesmen who drafted our Constitution, and a political culture that will sustain democratic authority and protect human freedom. But most nations that have become democracies lack some or all of these traits: There was no revolutionary war, few wise statesmen, and no democratic political culture in France, Germany, Italy, and Japan. England, the nation that became democratic a few decades after the United States was created, did have many helpful precursors: no feudalism, many independent farmers who owned their own land, and an early experience with an independent judiciary. England's former colonies—not only America, but Australia, Canada, India, and New Zealand—became the leading democracies of the world.

But other countries have become democratic despite internal terrorism (France), domestic autocracy (Germany), a weak political culture (Japan), a lack of territorial integrity (Italy), and a Muslim population (Turkey and increasingly Indonesia). The fact that not all democracies (in fact, almost none) will look like ours and that radicalism and despotism will make democratic progress painfully slow in many countries are not arguments against encouraging the spread of democracy; they are only arguments against hoping that our system can be exported intact and that we will see democracy in the most resistant nations in our (or our children's) lifetimes. Though American democracy got off to a good start in 1789, we had to fight a bloody civil war before much more progress could be made.

But we have left a legacy that many people wish to emulate. When people in Lebanon, Jordan, Morocco, and Indonesia are asked whether Western-style democracy can work in their countries, the overwhelming majority say "yes."

The greatest barrier to American influence on the world today is probably not our system of government or even our unequalled military power, but our popular culture. We export, to great individual but no collective applause, blue jeans, Big Macs, rock and hip-hop music, Web-based pornography, and motion pictures that often celebrate violence and a shallow adolescent culture. As Martha Bayles and others have pointed out, this is not what we exported right after the Second World War when, with government aid, we sent abroad artists, jazz musicians, and gifted writers to show what America could produce. Our earlier efforts at public diplomacy were a success; our most recent efforts at consumerism confirm in the minds of many leaders that we are a corrupt, violent, and mindless people.

There is a great irony in all this. Our foreign critics dislike the fact that freedom produces consumerism and ignore the fact that their followers buy into our retail output with great enthusiasm. In fact, despite our differences with other countries about capitalism, patriotism, and democracy, Americans generally share the same moral values as do people in Europe. As many Americans as foreigners are upset by the vulgarity of American motion pictures and video games. Anti-Americanism has deep roots, some linked to our foreign policies, some to our military power, and some merely to our vast impact on world affairs.

But much of it is dressed up to appear as a moral critique of America. Some of that is nonsense; movies starring Arnold Schwarzenegger, records featuring Frank Zappa, and fast-food restaurants penetrate to the farthest reaches of the globe, eagerly consumed by people who may wonder how a nation they are supposed to dislike produces so many things they love. Still, democracy and free enterprise encourages consumerism, and consumerism will lead to things that many people, notably in Muslim nations, will regard as immoral.

For our own good, I think America ought to lean against this picture of our country and encourage a renewed public diplomacy that emphasizes the deepest features of our culture: a love of freedom, a respect for great talent, and a willingness to forego any imperial ambitions even when we have the power to impose them. We did this after the Second World War by means of trips and broadcasts that drew on our best features. Today, as Martha Bayles has shown, we rely on the export of the basest forms of our popular culture. We cannot keep the latter at home, but we can do more to export the former.

(September 2006)

America's Democratization Projects Abroad

James Kurth

James Kurth examines the historical record regarding American efforts to promote democracy abroad and discovers a mixed record of some notable successes and numerous failures. The United States generally failed in its efforts to promote democracy in Latin America and Southeast Asia. He warns that the post-war successes in Germany and Japan, along with post-Cold War successes in Eastern Europe, do not provide useful models that can be applied to the Middle East. American-style liberal democracy, with its emphasis on individual rights and limited government, does not appear to be especially attractive as a governing model in developing nations. Instead, he cautions, different versions of illiberal democracy—majority rule without minority rights—are more likely to characterize the next wave of democratization in the world.

FOR ALMOST A CENTURY, the United States has been engaged in a succession of democratization projects abroad. President Woodrow Wilson in particular was an enthusiast in promoting democracy, first in the Caribbean basin and Central America ("I will teach the South Americans to elect good men") and then in Europe and beyond (the U.S. entry into World War I was supposed "to make the world safe for democracy").

Even earlier, during the nineteenth century, the United States had given rhetorical encouragement to democratic movements abroad, but it was not in a position to give them substantive support until it became a great power, a status that it achieved with its victory in the Spanish-American War of 1898. The Republican administrations of Theodore Roosevelt and William Howard Taft were quick to employ America's new power to promote regime change in the Caribbean basin, but their objective was merely to establish new governments that would make their countries safe for American security and business interests, i.e., regimes that certainly were liberal, but were not really democratic. With the Democratic administration of Woodrow Wilson, however, the United States embarked upon the promotion of democracy abroad in the full sense and in a big way. In the course of the twentieth century, there ensued a great parade of U.S. democratization projects that marched around the world.

THE SUCCESS STORIES

SOME OF THESE DEMOCRATIZATION projects were great successes. The most famous cases, of course, were Germany and Japan after their defeat in World War II, but these two examples (and exemplars) were joined by similar successes in Austria and Italy. In these four cases, of course, U.S.-style democratization was imposed by U.S.-led military occupation.

Also famous are the cases of Eastern Europe after the transformation—really, the defeat—of the Soviet Union in the Cold War. Here, of course, the United States did not impose a military occupation (but crucially the Soviets did withdraw theirs). Nevertheless, the result has been a wide swath of successful transitions to established liberal-democratic systems, stretching from the Baltic to the Balkans, or about a dozen countries in all. This has been a major achievement for U.S. foreign policy indeed.

Rather less sudden and dramatic, but still substantial and impressive, has been the U.S.-supported democratization of South Korea and Taiwan during the past two decades. Along with the earlier U.S.-imposed democratization of Japan, these two East Asian cases demonstrate that democratization projects can succeed not only in Europe (which, being part of Western civilization, might be expected to be receptive to liberal and democratic values), but also in at least one region beyond, one that has a very different cultural inheritance.

THE FAILURE STORIES

UNFORTUNATELY, OUR LONG PARADE of U.S. democratization projects includes some rather substantial failures as well. Not surprisingly, given the normal American tendency to be optimistic and to look upon the good side of some new project, these past failures are not nearly as famous as the past successes. They have been important, however, and they may be more relevant to the recent project of the Bush administration to democratize the Middle East and the Muslim world more generally. These past failures also raise cautions about any future U.S. effort to promote democracy in other regions as well.

Ironically, given the common and contemporary identification of democratization with "Wilsonianism," the original democratization projects of Woodrow Wilson himself *all* ended in failure. By the late 1920s, every country in Latin America where Wilson had employed U.S. military forces or other kind of intervention to teach the local citizens to elect good men had ended up with a military dictator or some other form of authoritarian regime. The same outcome occurred in Europe, where the consequences of failure would be much greater and much graver. Again, by 1930, almost every country in Eastern Europe where Wilson had employed U.S. pressure to bring about democratization—usually in the form of "self-determination"

—had ended up with some form of authoritarian regime. Democratic systems still remained in Germany, Austria, Czechoslovakia, and Finland, however, and it still could be said that Wilsonianism's achievements remained impressive. But then, with the onset and impact of the Great Depression, the democratic systems in Germany and Austria collapsed, and the consequences of these failures were more momentous and terrible than anything that could have been imagined.

What explains the failures of the original Wilsonian democratization projects? The most common factor—one characteristic of both the Latin American and the Eastern European failures in the 1920s—was the absence of a substantial middle class and, therefore, the presence of a large gap between a small upper class, largely composed of landlords and merchants, and a large lower class, most of whom were peasants. In contrast, in the Central European cases of Germany, Austria, and Czechoslovakia there was a very substantial middle class and a very substantial industrial working class as well, and these two classes continued to provide strong support for large democratic parties. Unfortunately, the Great Depression, which had a disastrous impact upon industrial production around the world, knocked the props out from this support, at least in Germany and Austria where democratic practices were relatively new. (We will have more to say about the supporting factors for democracy—and the differences between successes and failures—below.)

During the Cold War, the United States undertook a major democratization project in Southeast Asia, particularly in the Philippines in the 1950s–1960s and in South Vietnam in the 1960s. The epic U.S. military and political failure in South Vietnam (and in Cambodia and Laos as well) has cast this particular project into the darkest recesses of the American memory and has caused it to be largely forgotten. It would have been better to have remembered it, however, because some of the failed democratic initiatives tried in South Vietnam have been repeated and have failed in Iraq (e.g., expecting formal elections to solve fundamental conflicts). It should also be remembered that the U.S. project in the Philippines ended in the dictatorship of Ferdinand Marcos, which lasted from 1972 to 1986, when a democratic system of sorts was restored. Even today, however, Philippine democracy is afflicted by a large gap between a few rich and many poor, and the system remains fragile and fitful. In some ways, the Philippines can be seen as a kind of Latin Asia, bearing similarities to much of Latin America.

THE BUSH ADMINISTRATION'S FAILED PROJECT IN THE MIDDLE EAST

BEGINNING WITH THE DECLARATION of the Bush Doctrine in 2002 and with the invasion of Iraq in 2003, the Bush administration drove the United States into yet another democratization project in yet another foreign region, this time the Middle East and the Muslim world more generally. The rhetorical apotheosis of this particular project was President Bush's Second Inaugural Address in January 2005, and the highpoints of its apparent progress were the "Cedar Revolution" in Lebanon in 2005 and a series of hyped elections in Iraq in 2005 and 2006. Today, this project lies in ruins, destroyed by the Israel-Hezbollah war in Lebanon and the *de facto* civil war in Iraq (to say nothing of such results of democratic elections as the recent surge of votes for radical Islamists whenever they appear on the ballot, such as Hamas in Palestine and the Muslim Brotherhood in Egypt).

Is it possible that democratic elections in the Middle East and the Muslim world will actually have as their consequence the rise to power of "Islamofascism," the very totalitarian enemy that the Bush administration sought to defeat with its democratization project? If so, one should not be totally surprised, particularly if one is an administration that talks incessantly about the lessons the rest of us are supposed to learn from Nazi Germany. After all, it was successive free elections in the very democratic Weimar Republic after 1930 that brought the Nazis—the most extreme case of the original fascists—to power in 1933.

What lessons can be drawn from this record of successes and failures? Are there particular conditions that make a U.S. democratization project more likely to succeed (and also more likely to be worth its cost in the blood of American soldiers and the treasure of American citizens)? We will begin with an account of the legendary successes in Germany and Japan, along with the similar successes in Austria and Italy.

THE EXCEPTIONAL CASES FROM WORLD WAR II

FOR AMERICA, THE BIGGEST EVENT of the twentieth century was World War II. It is not surprising that the war's epic narrative has continued to shape the American public mentality (and political mythology), along with U.S. foreign policy, ever since. Munich and appeasement; Pearl Harbor and surprise attack; early 1942 and national desperation; later 1942 to 1945, resurgence and total victory; and, finally, the successful post-war democratization of our defeated enemies—each of these dramatic episodes in the World War II narrative has had a powerful hold on the American imagination. This largely explains why the successes of democratization in Germany and Japan have remained so salient and why Americans have easily been led into the temptation to think that those successes can be recapitulated elsewhere. The conditions that were common to those two cases (and also to the similar cases of Austria and Italy), however, have rarely been found in other times and in other regions. In particular, they are almost totally absent in the contemporary Middle East and most of the Muslim world.

Five conditions were important facilitators for the U.S. democratization projects in Germany, Japan, Austria, and Italy after World War II:

(1) *An industrial economy and a modern society.* Economic development in these four countries had reached the point that there was, as we noted above, a substantial middle class and industrial working class; in normal times, these had achieved their political representation in democratic political parties (liberal democratic in the case of the middle class, social democratic in the case of the working class).

Turning to the contemporary Middle East, we might think that several countries now have a substantial middle class (although clearly not an industrial working class). The economic wealth of Middle Eastern countries, however, is almost wholly the result of oil exports, and the middle class is largely found among the employees in the state sector. It is a dependent and unproductive middle class, rather than the independent and productive one that characterized Central Europe and Japan; the former provides a weak and unstable basis for liberal democracy.

(2) *A prior liberal-democratic experience.* Our second condition flows out of the first. Democratic parties had already existed in these four countries in the 1920s and, in some cases, even in earlier decades, i.e., before the Great Depression (Germany, Austria, and Japan) or other social conflicts (Italy) brought about the collapse of the liberal-democratic system and the advent of an authoritarian regime. This meant that the United States in the late 1940s could reach back and build upon democratic memories, practices, and even particular leaders from the earlier democratic era.

In this respect, the contrast of our four post-war cases with the contemporary Middle East could hardly be greater. Hardly any Middle Eastern country has ever been a liberal democracy (Turkey and perhaps Lebanon are arguable exceptions); in one country after another, there is no historical base or precedent whatsoever for the U.S. democratization project.

(3) *Total military defeat.* In 1945, the old authoritarian regimes had been totally defeated militarily by the United States and its

allies. As a consequence, they had been totally discredited ideologically. This opened up a great political space that could be filled by the liberal-democratic ideology of the victorious United States.

One might argue that Saddam Hussein's regime experienced a similar military defeat and ideological discrediting in 2003. The Sunni population of Iraq, however, which was tied so closely to the Baath regime, obviously does not agree. Military defeat is not the term that comes to mind when we are describing the Sunni insurgency in Iraq. Moreover, since the U.S. military is now so tied down and stretched so thin in Iraq, there is no prospect whatever that it will be able totally to defeat and occupy another Middle Eastern country, as it did with the enemy countries in World War II.

(4) *A greater foreign threat.* Of course, the populations of the defeated countries disliked their occupation by the U.S. Army. However, they feared a potential occupation by the Soviet Army even more, and it soon became clear to them it was the U.S. Army that provided the best protection against a Soviet invasion, or against a Soviet-supported Communist revolution.

Some semblance of this condition is also present in Iraq. The Kurds fear a threat posed by Turkey, but they fear the Sunnis of Iraq even more. This is why they have been such close and cooperative allies of the United States. The Sunnis themselves are coming to view the Shiites of Iraq as their greatest enemy, but they continue to loathe the U.S. military forces as well. As for the Shiites, it is possible that one day they might come to fear a threat posed by Sunni Saudi Arabia or even by Shiite Iran. For now, however, they fear the Iraqi Sunnis most of all, and their militias are also verging on a conflict with the U.S. military. All in all, the complex array of foreign threats in Iraq does not wonderfully concentrate Iraqi minds in the way the Soviet threat did in our four cases after World War II.

(5) *An ethnically homogeneous population.* This fifth condition may be the most relevant to the contrast between the four post-war successes and the contemporary Middle East. Although these four

countries were certainly divided by class conflicts, they were, in ethnic terms, among the most homogenous societies in the world. There was very little prospect that one ethnic group, especially one located in a distinct territory, would try to secede from the rest of the country.

The contrast with the contemporary Middle East, and particularly with Iraq, again could not be greater. As is now well-known (and was always well-known to scholars of Middle Eastern politics and society), Iraq has never been ethnically homogeneous; from its creation in 1920, it has always been divided into three ethnic parts, the Sunni Arabs, the Shiite Arabs, and the Kurds (who are Sunni, but non-Arab), with the Sunni minority until 2003 imposing an authoritarian and usually brutal regime upon the Shiite majority and the Kurdish minority. Moreover, the three ethnic parts have roughly corresponded to three territorial parts, with the Sunni Arabs in the center, the Shiite Arabs in the south, and the Kurds in the north (with mixed populations in major cities). Iraq was always an unstable equilibrium, a partition waiting to happen, artificially held together by the iron bonds of an authoritarian and brutal regime. In such circumstances, "regime change" would inevitably result in state change or even country change; in particular democratization would mean that one or more of the three ethnic and territorial parts of Iraq would vote to separate itself from the others. One could have an Iraq, but without democracy. Alternatively, one could have democracy, but without an Iraq. But one could not have both.

To get some sense of what democratization could produce in a country with such pronounced ethnic heterogeneity, one would have had to look not at West Germany and Japan in the late 1940s but instead at the recent (and very extensive) experience of democratization in the former Communist countries. Certainly, one would have to especially look at the experience of democratization in the Balkans, which was once called the Near East and which is not that far geographically and sociologically from the contemporary Middle East.

Here, the evidence is unambiguous. In virtually every country in the Communist world where there was ethnic heterogeneity, democratization (which included free elections) was followed immediately by secession and partition. This was largely peaceful in the case of the Slavic and the Baltic republics of the Soviet Union and in the case of the "velvet divorce" between the Czech Republic and the Slovak Republic. It was violent and even genocidal in the case of the Caucasian republics of the Soviet Union and in the case of several of the republics of Yugoslavia. But whether the process be peaceful or violent, the democratization of multiethnic societies almost always issued in secession and partition. Given these results of democratization in multiethnic countries of the Communist world in the 1990s—especially the violent results in the Caucasus and the Balkans, which are so proximate to Iraq both geographically and historically—it is incredible that anyone could seriously argue that the most relevant comparisons to Iraq were the homogeneous nations of West Germany and Japan in the 1940s. When neoconservative writers did so, they were therefore either frauds or fools.

THE PERVASIVENESS OF ETHNIC DIVISIONS IN THE MUSLIM WORLD

ETHNIC DIVISIONS AND CONFLICTS are especially pronounced in Iraq, but they are seen throughout the Muslim world. This has important implications for any democratization project there. In appearance, a common faith in Islam unites Muslim countries; the ideal of Islam is that the Muslim world forms one great Islamic community or nation, known as the *umma*. In reality, however, this appearance of Islamic unity lies atop a myriad of ethnic and tribal divisions that existed before Islam (especially in Muhammad's own Arabia) and that have never been eliminated by Islam. Indeed, one might interpret the Muslim world's intense proclamation of unity as rhetorical compensation for persistent conflict among a multitude of ethnic communities or tribes.

Almost all Muslim countries are really multiethnic or multitribal societies, usually composed of one large ethnic community plus several smaller ones. Often, each ethnic community is concentrated in a particular region of the country. The actual basis for most political behavior in Muslim countries is these ethnic or tribal communities; most people act to preserve or promote the interests of their own ethnic community or tribe against the interests of other ones. Very little sense of the public interest or the common good exists in Muslim countries; left alone, these communities or tribes would war with each other despite the purported unity of Islam.

In most cases, one ethnic community or tribe imposes a peace of sorts on the others and then becomes strong enough to form a state. Given the condition of persistent and pervasive ethnic and tribal conflict, this state will be authoritarian—a Hobbesian Leviathan. As we have seen, this pattern of a uni-ethnic state ruling over a multiethnic or multitribal society clearly characterized Saddam Hussein's Iraq. Similarly, before being ousted by the United States in 2001, the Taliban regime in Afghanistan represented the domination of the Pashtuns over several other ethnic groups. This pattern also exists in contemporary Iran, Syria, and Sudan, and some version of it exists in Pakistan, Indonesia, Saudi Arabia, Yemen, Algeria, and many other Muslim countries as well. When the ruling community is especially small, it compensates for weakness in its numbers by extreme brutality in its repressive measures (e.g., Baathist Iraq and Syria). In any case, the multiethnic society is held together and held down by a uniethnic state, particularly by its security apparatus.

These Muslim political systems are really small multinational empires. Indeed, they are governed in ways similar to those that the Ottomans used to govern their empire. The Ottoman Turks provided the state or "ruling institution" that kept a wide variety of ethnic communities or "millets" (some Muslim and some non-Muslim) operating within one imperial system. A millet often served a distinct economic or social function; the function of the Ottoman Turks was to rule the rest. The Ottoman Empire ended more than eighty years ago, but its basic pattern lives on in most contemporary Muslim countries, which remain miniature and stunted versions of the old Ottoman imperial system, with the contemporary state security apparatus playing the ruling-institution role. The members of the different ethnic communities under the ruling state do not see themselves as citizens who enjoy equal rights within one homogenous nation. Instead, they see themselves as distinct tribes or ethnic groups, at most a collection of nations within a nation but not of it, or a nation within an empire. This is hardly a promising basis for a viable liberal democracy.

Such multiethnic society/uniethnic state contraptions are inherently unstable. They are accidents, secessions, and partitions waiting to happen. Whenever the state is suddenly and sharply weakened (as with Iran during the Revolution of 1979 and with Iraq during the Gulf War of 1991 and during the Iraq war since 2003), the subordinate ethnic communities try to break away from what they see to be a brutal but now-failed empire. Since these communities are concentrated in particular regions, their efforts amount to secession. The multiethnic empire survives when a new or renewed brutal state security apparatus is constructed, which then puts down the secession. Of course, in contemporary Iraq, the United States, because of the very nature of its democratization project, has prevented the construction of any such security apparatus. The result is an Iraq that is neither a multiethnic empire nor a liberal democracy, but merely an ongoing anarchy amounting to a civil war.

IDEALISTS VERSUS REALISTS

THE PERENNIAL U.S. EFFORTS at democratization abroad have given rise to a perennial debate over U.S. foreign policy—the famous and long-standing debate between "idealists" and "realists." As it happens, each of these two camps can make a useful contribution to our examination into the successes and failures of U.S. democratization projects. Unfortunately, it is also the case that each camp can lead us into serious errors as well.

In their pure form, idealists neglect the historical record of the failed projects, and they therefore ignore the lessons that might be drawn from these failures. This kind of behavior has certainly been true of the promoters of the recent U.S. project in the Middle East. The idealists also neglect the historical record in another sense: they normally ignore the cultural and social particularities—and therefore the realities—of the countries which they seek to democratize. This too has been a characteristic of the promoters of the recent project in the Middle East. The most pronounced examples of this willful ignorance of cultural, social, and historical particularities have been the neoconservatives, especially (and most consequentially) in their writings on Iraq.

Indeed, the idealists normally ignore the cultural and social particularities of America itself. The neoconservatives are always talking about America being a "propositional nation" (i.e., one based upon universal ideals and with no distinctive, inherited ethnic or even national identity), as if Americans were all intellectuals engaged in discourse and debates about propositions, like the neoconservatives themselves. But, of course, most Americans have their own very real, immediate, and particular ethnic identities and economic interests, and they normally do not see these identities and interests advanced by abstract (and bloody and costly) democratization projects abroad. This is why the Bush administration's (and the neoconservatives') project in Iraq has been left with virtually no support within the American public.

Conversely, in their pure form, realists neglect the historical record of the successful democratization projects, and they therefore overlook countries where conditions have developed that could facilitate democratization in the future. This kind of failure of imagination led realists in the 1980s to be skeptical of the real potential for successful democratization in most of Eastern Europe.

Their focus on past cultural, social, and historical particularities led them to assume that the dismal political history of the region could only be repeated. By the 1980s, however, the economic development of much of Eastern Europe had created social and economic conditions comparable to those reached in Central Europe several decades before, i.e., by the 1920s. In addition, the growing connections between Communist Eastern Europe and liberal-democratic Western Europe made the liberal-democratic alternative seem both very attractive and very feasible.

Moreover, and ironically, the realists normally neglect a cultural and social particularity of America itself, and that is the fact that virtually any major U.S. foreign policy has to be legitimated with some kind of democratic rhetoric. This is a necessary part of bringing certain groups (especially liberal professionals and professional liberals) into a grand coalition to support the policy. Finally, a fundamental reality about America's position in the world is that in general U.S. national interests are indeed best served and advanced when other states become established liberal democracies.

A DIFFERENT KIND OF DEMOCRATIZATION: ILLIBERAL DEMOCRACY

DEMOCRATIZATION IN THE MIDDLE EAST is now obviously a failed project. Is it possible, however, that there are other regions where democratization might still have a promising future? As it happens, there is one such region, and that is Latin America. The form democratization is most likely to take there, however, will not be similar to the American one, i.e., *liberal* democracy, complete with some kind of separation of powers, constitutionalism, rule of law, and minority rights. It is more likely to be what Fareed Zakaria has called "illiberal democracy," particularly *populist* democracy, marked perhaps by generally free elections but also by presidential dominance, pervasive executive discretion, and majority rule.

Populist, or illiberal, democracy seems to be a natural political tendency, and a perennial political system, in much of Latin America. It has certainly returned in a big way in that region in the 2000s, replacing the more liberal-democratic regimes of the 1990s (which were often derided as imposing "neo-liberalism" and "the Washington Consensus" on their citizens and on behalf of U.S. interests). The most extreme versions of populism now rule in Venezuela and Bolivia, but some version of populist democracy now prevails in Argentina, Chile, Uruguay, and perhaps Brazil. Populist movements also recently came close to electoral victory in Mexico and Peru. All in all, Latin America has been swept by a major wave of populist democracy in the past few years.

Populism in Latin America is also anti-"imperialist," which means that it is usually anti-American. As with Islamism in the Middle East, free elections in Latin America are now putting into power governments that resent or even loathe the United States. If America were not now bogged down in its grueling war in Iraq, U.S. policy makers and the American media would forever be talking about the populist threat in Latin America.

In the fullness of time, the recurring economic and social failures of populist democracy will probably discredit it, just as the failures of liberal democracy have recently discredited that political alternative. Some new (or renewed) system will then arise in Latin America, perhaps yet another variation on an authoritarian theme. But it will probably be at least a generation before we see a revival of the distinctively American project of liberal democracy in Latin America.

A DIFFERENT KIND OF LIBERALISM: LIBERAL UNDEMOCRACY

IF DEMOCRATIZATION WITHOUT LIBERALISM is the likely future for Latin America, is there a place where we might hope for the obverse, i.e., liberalism without democracy, or liberal undemocracy, so to speak? After all, most Western European countries passed through this stage in the nineteenth century on their path from authoritarian monarchy to liberal democracy. As it happens, there is indeed one very large country where a phase of liberal undemocracy is a reasonable prospect—China.

The extremely rapid economic development of China over the past two decades has produced a new, and numerous, middle class, and, like the classical European and American middle classes, the Chinese middle class is largely independent and certainly productive. For many practical purposes, the Chinese Communist Party has devolved economic decision-making to a new and dynamic elite of entrepreneurs. Moreover, there is now a very well-educated, but also very sensible, professional sector. But entrepreneurs and professionals normally seek the legal and political stability and predictability that come with the expansion of the rule of law and constitutionalism. Historically, these two sectors have formed a strong constituency for liberal institutions, even if these institutions are not yet really democratic, and they do so in China today.

The Chinese entrepreneurs and professionals have become essential, indeed central, to China's developmental path, and the Communist regime understands and accepts this. Because of the vigorous push of these entrepreneurs and professionals for the rule of law and even constitutionalism, the prospects are good that China will move progressively—albeit in fits and starts—toward a more liberal regime. If so, China will follow along a path taken in earlier decades by other East Asian countries, in particular Japan, Taiwan, and South Korea. Because of the vast size and diversity of China, however, full democracy itself would probably unleash a variety of centrifugal tendencies and secessionist movements. At least, this is what the Chinese Communist Party firmly believes. The road to democracy in China will be far more rocky and risky than it was in the much smaller and more homogenous countries of Japan, Taiwan, and South Korea. Consequently, we are not going to get truly democratic institutions in China anytime soon, even though we may soon see some truly liberal institutions there—in short, liberal undemocracy.

IS THERE ANY FUTURE FOR LIBERAL DEMOCRATIZATION?

FINALLY, DESPITE THE SOMBER ANALYSIS, the dismal science, that we have offered in this essay, is there any place where there can be progress in the future in the direction of good old, American-style, liberal democracy? Perhaps the place to look is near where there has been such dramatic progress in that direction in the recent past. Certainly, the grand narrative of post-Communist Eastern Europe represents one of the most striking successes of full democratization, and liberal democratization at that. Is it possible that the region immediately to the south and the east of Eastern Europe (which now is once again better thought of as Central Europe) might provide the next chapter in the success story of liberal democratization?

At the moment, this region does not seem very promising. Illiberal, particularly populist, democracy seems to be the most prevalent political tendency in much of the contemporary Balkans, specifically in Romania, Bulgaria, Serbia, and Macedonia. These countries are democratic in the sense that they have free elections, but they are hardly characterized by stable and effective political institutions or by the rule of law. Further east, something similar seems to prevail in Ukraine, the locale of the "orange" revolution, in which popular demonstrations brought about regime change, but the new government has turned out to be ineffective and unstable.

Much of the populations of these countries want to become members of the European Union, however, and indeed Romania and Bulgaria are scheduled to do so next year. But the E.U. is exerting great pressure upon these countries, as a condition for membership, to strengthen the rule of law, constitutionalism, and liberal institutions generally. The struggle between populist democracy and liberal democracy will likely be the main story in this region over the next decade.

It will be a story, however, whose major author will be the European Union, and not the United States. The E.U., closer to this region in almost every sense—geographical, economic, and cultural—will be both necessary and sufficient to make this one more success story for liberal-democratization projects. The United States, remote in almost every sense, has very little that it can add (although with its perennial, crude over-simplifications, it can subtract). And so, it seems that, as we look around the world and peer into the future, we can discern a variety of ongoing democratic and liberal projects— populist democracy, liberal undemocracy, and even liberal democracy. But in regard to any traditional U.S. democratization project, we can now discern nothing in the future at all.

(October 2006)

A Masterpiece
of American Oratory

Norman Podhoretz

In Norman Podhoretz's view, George W. Bush's Second Inaugural Address remains wildly underestimated, underappreciated, and misunderstood. In this essay, he assesses the Inaugural Address as a ringing articulation of America's indispensable purpose in the world, comparing it favorably to earlier addresses by Presidents Roosevelt, Truman, Kennedy, and Reagan. In his view, the Bush Doctrine—the idea that the United States has a duty to promote democracy and free institutions in the world—is fully in keeping with the foreign policy tradition of the nation. In time, he argues, President Bush's Second Inaugural Address will be acclaimed as "a masterpiece of American oratory, worthy of a place beside Lincoln's Second Inaugural."

GEORGE W. BUSH has been "misunderestimated" so many times that this sardonic neologism has forced its way into the American language and will forever be associated with his name. Yet never has the judgment of his performance been so wildly off the mark as in the response to his Second Inaugural Address. Naturally his political enemies were quick to deride the speech. But this time a large contingent of his conservative supporters also joined in the cacophonous chorus of denigration.

What brought all this wrath down on the Second Inaugural was the President's decision to use it as an occasion for reaffirming and rededicating both himself and the nation to the ideas he had embraced in the wake of 9/11 and that have collectively come to be known as the Bush Doctrine. But rather than taking us step by step through its various components, as he had done in a number of previous (and equally misunderestimated) speeches, he now redoubled the provocation by subsuming them all into "the ultimate goal of ending tyranny in our world."

Having for my part listened with growing awe to the President as he showed how this goal grows out of the moral and spiritual imperatives of the American past, how it confronts the urgencies of the American present, and how it ensures the security of the American future, and then having confirmed my immediate reaction by repeated readings of the text, I was astonished by what the conservative commentariat had to say about the speech in the days immediately following its delivery.

Of course I knew very well that some eminent conservatives—most notably William F. Buckley Jr. and George Will—had all along been discreetly uneasy about the Bush Doctrine, and particularly the element of it he singled out for special emphasis in this speech. I was also well aware that a faction existed on the right whose most prominent member was Patrick J. Buchanan and whose view of the Bush Doctrine went beyond uneasiness into an outspoken hostility that could hardly be exceeded even by the sheer hatred pervading the left. Consequently I was not in the least surprised to find both of these groups expressing dismay over the substance of the speech. Still, because they were both led by people who were very good writers themselves and who had also been capable in the past of appreciating good writing even when produced by their political opponents, I was a bit surprised by their (willful?) blindness to its literary qualities.

Even more surprising was that the same blindness had afflicted several supporters of the Bush Doctrine like David Frum, Peter Robinson, and Peggy Noonan who, as former presidential speechwriters themselves, might also have been expected to recognize literary distinction when it was staring them in the face. Yet Frum dismissed the speech as "a disappointing work" with "high fat content" that should have been reduced by careful editing; Robinson grudgingly conceded that it was "well written" and "in places actually beautiful," but on the whole it made him "mighty nervous"; and for Noonan, too, its "moments of eloquence" were overwhelmed by "high-class boilerplate" and "over the top" rhetoric that left her "with a bad feeling and reluctant dislike."

WITH THESE CRITICISMS IN MIND, I have just read the speech yet again, and I am more convinced than ever that it will ultimately be acclaimed as a masterpiece of American oratory, worthy of a place beside Lincoln's Second Inaugural—which, incidentally, was also widely derided immediately after being delivered. To the *New York Herald*, it was "a little speech of 'glittering generalities' used only to fill in the program," and the *Chicago Times* "did not conceive it possible that even Mr. Lincoln could produce a paper so slip shod, so loose-jointed, so puerile . . . in literary construction. . . ." To us today such judgments seem puzzling, and even laughable, and so, I believe, will it some day be the case with the attacks on Bush's Second Inaugural.

Whatever may have been true of Lincoln's critics, those who were sour about Bush's Second Inaugural for stylistic reasons must suddenly, and most mysteriously, have developed a tin ear for English prose. Otherwise how could they have been deaf to the exquisite rhetorical flourishes that (far from being "over the top") never exceed the bounds of the best literary taste? How could they have failed to hear the rhythmical sureness of the language? How could they not have reverberated to the incantatory beauty of the cadences?

Take this dazzling passage, which comes right after the introductory formalities, and thus sets the tone for everything that is to follow:

At this second gathering, our duties are defined not by the words I use, but by the history we have seen together. For half a century, America defended our own freedom by standing watch on distant borders. After the shipwreck of Communism came years of relative quiet, years of repose, years of sabbatical—and then there came a day of fire.

In its diction and pitch, "years of repose, years of sabbatical" is perfect as a lyrical gloss on "relative quiet" and as a prelude to the sudden shock of "—and then there came a day of fire." Fire then turns out to be one of the unifying images of the speech. Here, it obviously refers to 9/11, but when the President picks it up again later in another and even more marvelous passage, he uses it to remind us that we have turned this fire back and proudly put it to exactly the opposite purpose for which it was set off against us on that terrible day:

> Our country has accepted obligations that are difficult to fulfill, and would be dishonorable to abandon. Yet because we have acted in the great liberating tradition of this nation, tens of millions have achieved their freedom. And as hope kindles hope, millions more will find it. By our efforts we have lit a fire as well—a fire in the minds of men. It warms those who feel its power, it burns those who fight its progress, and one day this untamed fire of freedom will reach the darkest corners of our world.

Note how the rhetoric here steadily mounts in intensity while remaining securely within the confines of restraint, and note too how the rhythmic beat reinforces the idea being conveyed. Note also how the image of fire is developed through an organic and inexorable progression: first it "kindles," then it "warms," then it "burns," and finally, in a triumphant crescendo, it blazes so "untamed" that it can light up "the darkest corners of our world."

This is a level of literary power that can only be reached by a writer in total command of his material and absolutely faithful to its own inner demands.

SO MUCH, then, for the charges against the speech as a piece of writing: they are no less ridiculous than those the *Chicago Times* hurled against the "literary construction" of Lincoln's Second Inaugural. But making itself even more ridiculous, the *Chicago Times* added that "in its ideas, its sentiments, its grasp," Lincoln's speech was also "slip shod, loose-jointed, and puerile." In my opinion, the analogous charges that have been made against the substance of Bush's Second Inaugural are—and will in time be seen—as equally preposterous.

Let me begin with the least credible of these charges—that there is, as the headline of Peggy Noonan's piece in the *Wall Street Journal* put it, "way too much God" in the speech. I for one—but not by any means I alone—was taken aback to see this criticism coming from Peggy Noonan, who has never previously been notable for complaining about expressions of religious faith in the public square. Be that as it may, by my count there are five references to God here (one of them within a quote from Lincoln), as compared with eight, plus several extended citations from the Bible, in Lincoln's own Second Inaugural (which, interestingly, was itself attacked by the *New York World* for "abandoning all pretense of statesmanship" and taking "refuge in piety"). I have not gone through all the other inaugural addresses in American history, but I would guess that they all contain at least as many invocations of God as Bush's did. (John F. Kennedy's has four, plus a verse from the prophet Isaiah.) Measured by what standard, then, is there "way too much" in Bush's Second Inaugural?

Another frequently registered objection is that the speech overreaches—that in promising to end tyranny everywhere in the world it sets forth a goal which is far too ambitious and uses language which is far too universalist. This is a more serious criticism, and yet, as with the one about too much God, it is hard to see in what way Bush is any more ambitious and universalist than his major twentieth-century predecessors, either in their own Inaugural Addresses or in speeches on other crucially important occasions.

The most obvious example is Woodrow Wilson, who promised to "make the world safe for democracy" by sending Americans to fight in World War I. True, the horrors and then the disillusioning aftermath of that war helped to discredit Wilson's slogan. But that did not prevent Franklin D. Roosevelt, the next Democrat to win the presidency, from going even further in preparing the nation for an eventual entry into World War II:

> We look forward to a world founded upon four essential human freedoms.
>
> The first is freedom of speech and expression—everywhere in the world.
>
> The second is freedom of every person to worship God in his own way—everywhere in the world.
>
> The third is freedom from want . . .—everywhere in the world.
>
> The fourth is freedom from fear . . .—anywhere in the world.

Next we come to Roosevelt's successor, Harry S. Truman. Like Bush, Truman was at first regarded as a mediocre politician with no interest in and no grasp of foreign policy. But as he watched the Soviet Union forcing Communist regimes on more and more countries in East Europe while also using local Communist parties to subvert countries in other parts of the world, Truman (again like Bush after 9/11) amazed everyone by rising to the challenge.

It all began on March 12, 1947, when he appealed to Congress for aid to Greece and Turkey, both of which, he said, were threatened by Soviet-led "movements that seek to impose upon them totali-

tarian regimes." He was, he went on, "fully aware of the broad implications involved if the United States extends assistance to Greece
and Turkey," and in spelling these out he enunciated the main principle of what soon was being called the Truman Doctrine:

> At the present moment in world history nearly every nation
> must choose between alternative ways of life. The choice is too
> often not a free one.
>
> Our way of life is based upon the will of the majority, and
> is distinguished by free institutions, representative government,
> free elections, guarantees of individual freedom, freedom of
> speech and religion, and freedom from political oppression.
>
> The second way of life is based upon the will of a minority
> forcibly imposed upon the majority. It relies upon terror and
> oppression, a controlled press and radio; fixed elections, and
> the suppression of personal freedoms.
>
> I believe that it must be the policy of the United States to
> support free peoples who are resisting attempted subjugation
> by armed minorities or by outside pressures.

Fourteen years later, on January 20, 1961, John F. Kennedy, like
FDR in relation to Wilson, went Truman one better:

> Let every nation know, whether it wishes us well or ill, that we
> shall pay any price, bear any burden, meet any hardship, sup-
> port any friend, oppose any foe, to assure the survival and the
> success of liberty.

These were the most famous words Kennedy was ever to utter,
but in connection with the criticisms of Bush's Second Inaugural
as containing too much God and for universalizing the hunger for
freedom, it is worth quoting the much less familiar passage that led
up to them:

I have sworn before you and Almighty God the same solemn
oath our forebears prescribed nearly a century and three quar-
ters ago. The world is very different now.... And yet the same
revolutionary beliefs for which our forebears fought are still at
issue around the globe—the belief that the rights of man come
not from the generosity of the state, but from the hand of God.

In Bush's Second Inaugural, echoes can be heard of all these
speeches, and by drawing in this fashion on three of his Democratic
predecessors, he is subtly suggesting that there is nothing narrowly
partisan about his own Doctrine. Watch how delicately he plays
on some of the pronouncements quoted above without ever men-
tioning the names of their authors:

We are led, by events and common sense, to one conclusion:
The survival of liberty in our land increasingly depends on the
success of liberty in other lands. The best hope for peace in our
world is the expansion of freedom in all the world.

The second sentence evokes Roosevelt, the first plucks the Kennedy string, and the passage about fire I quoted above also harks
back to—and greatly improves on—this one from Kennedy:

The energy, the faith, the devotion which we bring to this
endeavor will light our country and all who serve it—and the
glow from that fire can truly light the world.

Traces of Truman also appear, as in Bush's declaration

that it is the policy of the United States to seek and support
the growth of democratic movements and institutions in every
nation and culture....

BUT WHAT OF REPUBLICAN predecessors? There are those—and they can be found within both the old foreign-policy establishment and the conservative camp—who deny that the Bush Doctrine is true to the traditions of the Republican Party. In fact, going so far as even to deny that (as Bush and others, myself included, often claim) it builds on the legacy of Ronald Reagan, they argue that, on the contrary, it veers off onto a radically different path. No doubt it is with this argument in mind that Bush makes very sure to add an unmistakable echo of Reagan to the ghostly choir of the three Democrats he has assembled.

Here is Reagan, speaking at Westminster Abbey on June 8, 1982:

> We must be staunch in our conviction that freedom is not the
> sole prerogative of a lucky few, but the inalienable and universal
> right of all human beings. . . . It would be cultural condescen-
> sion, or worse, to say that any people prefer dictatorship to
> democracy.

And here is Bush's version of the same point:

> Some, I know, have questioned the global appeal of liberty—
> though . . . Americans, of all people, should never be surprised
> by the power of our ideals. Eventually the call of freedom comes
> to every mind and every soul. . . . America will not pretend that
> jailed dissidents prefer their chains, or that women welcome
> humiliation and servitude, or that any human being aspires to
> live at the mercy of bullies.

Above even Reagan, however, it is Abraham Lincoln—the greatest Republican of them all, and the greatest of all American Presidents—whose spirit hovers most brightly over the face of Bush's

Second Inaugural. Lincoln, indeed, is the only one he quotes directly and by name:

> The rulers of outlaw regimes know that we still believe as
> Abraham Lincoln did: "Those who deny freedom to others
> deserve it not for themselves; and, under the rule of a just God,
> cannot long retain it."

But there are also many unattributed echoes of Lincoln throughout this speech. For example, on Lincoln's "As I would not be a slave, so I would not be a master. This expresses my idea of democracy," Bush composes this variation:

> Across the generations we have proclaimed the imperative of
> self-government, because no one is fit to be a master, and no
> one deserves to be a slave.

Another example is the creative adaptation by Bush of Lincoln's summation of the "real issue" of his debates with Stephen Douglas. Lincoln:

> It is the eternal struggle between these two principles—right
> and wrong—throughout the world. They are the two principles
> that have stood face to face from the beginning of time; and will
> ever continue to struggle. . . . No matter in what shape it comes,
> whether from the mouth of a king who seeks to bestride the
> people of his own nation and live by the fruit of their labor, or
> from one race of men as an apology for enslaving another race,
> it is the same tyrannical principle.

Now Bush:

> We will persistently clarify the choice before every ruler and
> every nation: The moral choice between oppression, which is
> always wrong, and freedom, which is eternally right.

YET TO DEMOSTRATE even more definitively that his own Doctrine is rooted deep in American soil, Bush reaches not only beyond his twentieth-century predecessors of both parties and back to Lincoln; he even goes beyond Lincoln and all the way back to the Declaration of Independence. In this he must have been inspired by Lincoln himself, who, in maintaining that slavery was wrong, appealed over the head of the Constitution (by which slavery was permitted) to the Declaration of Independence (by which it was logically forbidden):

> I believe the declaration that "all men are created equal" is the great fundamental principle upon which our free institutions rest.

Bush similarly bases what he calls "our deepest beliefs" as Americans on the Declaration, where it is further asserted of "all men" that "they are endowed by their Creator with certain inalienable rights." Bush:

> From the day of our Founding, we have proclaimed that every man and woman on this earth has rights, and dignity, and matchless value, because they bear the image of the Maker of Heaven and earth.

And he returns to the Declaration in a beautiful peroration which is also Lincoln-like in the biblical music it makes and its play on a biblical verse:

> When the Declaration of Independence was first read in public and the Liberty Bell was sounded in celebration, a witness said: "It rang as if it meant something." In our time it means something still. America, in this young century, proclaims liberty throughout all the world, and to all the inhabitants thereof. Renewed in our strength—tested, but not weary—we are ready for the greatest achievements in the history of freedom.

If, then, Bush is guilty of excessive universalizing in his Second Inaugural, he has plenty of presidential company, including both the founder of the Republican Party in the nineteenth century and the greatest Republican president of the twentieth.

EVEN SO, given the relentless attacks by Democrats on the Bush Doctrine in general and on this speech in particular, it should be pointed out that the rhetoric of the three Democrats with whom this Republican President associates himself was if anything much more far-reaching in its universalism than his own. After all, Roosevelt asserted that to all human beings *"everywhere in the world"* no fewer than four freedoms were "essential" (even, remarkably, freedom from fear), but Bush speaks only of freedom from political and religious tyranny; and whereas Roosevelt thought he could deliver all four of these freedoms not in "a distant millennium" but "in our own time and generation," Bush recognizes that "The great objective of ending tyranny is the concentrated work of generations."

Admittedly Truman was a bit less sweeping than Roosevelt had been before him; he did not add "everywhere" to the "free peoples" it would be his policy to support. Still, in moving from Greece and Turkey to "nearly every nation" in the world, he was sweeping enough to alarm Walter Lippmann, the most admired columnist of the day, who wrote:

> A vague global policy, which sounds like the tocsin of an ideological crusade, has no limits.... Everyone everywhere will read into it his own fears and hopes....

Nor did Hans J. Morgenthau, then the leading theorist of *Realpolitik* in the academic world, pay any heed to the gestures of caution in Truman's speech, which he denounced for having transformed a concrete interest of the United States in a geographically defined part of the world into a moral principle of worldwide validity, to be applied regardless of the limits of American interest and power.

Bush introduces some of the same qualifications into his speech as Truman did. Like Truman ("I believe that we must assist free peoples to work out their own destinies in their own way"), Bush insists that "Our goal . . . is to help others find their own voice, attain their own freedom, and make their own way." Like Truman, too (who stressed aid over military action, but who was soon to show, by going into Korea, that he was prepared to use force when nothing else would avail), Bush believes that the goal of ending tyranny ". . . is not primarily the task of arms, though we will defend ourselves and our friends by force of arms when necessary."

Not that such qualifications proved any more effective than Truman's did as a defense against attack from today's disciples of Lippmann in the media and of Morgenthau in the academy, let alone from the isolationists and the non-interventionists who still exist, as they also did then, on the left as well as the right.

And if Bush never goes as far as Roosevelt did, and no further than Truman, he is much more restrained than Kennedy was. Certainly there is nothing in his Second Inaugural to match the overkill of Kennedy's "pay any price, bear any burden" passage.

In short, the accusations of overreach that have been thrown at Bush's speech simply do not stand up when we look at it in the context of the oratorical American tradition out of which it flows. But this still leaves us with the question of how we are to understand his universalist language in the context of the present political situation. How does it square with the praise he has lavished on Vladimir Putin, even though the Russian leader has reversed the progress toward democratization that his country seemed to be making after the fall of Communism? How does it fit with the soft policy he has followed toward China, whose government remains politically repressive even though its economy has become relatively free? And what about the virtual alliance he has made with the Pakistani dictator Pervez Musharraf? In the eyes of some, cases like this expose Bush's universalist rhetoric as empty and/or hypocritical.

YET SURELY THESE CRITICS must—or at any rate should—know that, just as the Nazis and fascists were the main and immediate target in World War II, and just as the Communists were the main and immediate target in World War III (the Cold War), so our main and immediate target in what I persist in calling World War IV is the Islamofascist terrorists and the Middle Eastern despotisms by which they are bred, sheltered, financed, and armed.

Surely, too, Bush's critics must, or should, know that when Roosevelt held out the hope of spreading the four freedoms "everywhere in the world," it was clear to all sides that he was challenging only the Axis powers, and not the equally totalitarian Soviet Union or any of the smaller fascist regimes in other parts of the world; nor did anyone think that his willingness to forge an alliance with Stalin meant that he was spouting empty rhetoric or being hypocritical.

Similarly, when Truman promised to come to the aid of "free peoples resisting attempted subjugation," and when Kennedy spoke of opposing "any foe," everyone recognized that they were talking about the Soviet Union and the Communist regimes and parties controlled by or allied with it. Nor did anyone (not even Lippmann and Morgenthau) seriously imagine that they were preparing to dislodge every tyrant and every dictator on the face of the earth or, conversely, that this prudential limitation exposed the universalism of their language as nothing but rodomontade.

Finally—as Republican critics of Bush must or should know—their party had little if anything to say against Reagan when (in complete fidelity to the Truman Doctrine but in clear violation of his own universalist declarations) he adopted a policy of supporting authoritarian regimes that were threatened either directly or indirectly by the much worse totalitarianism of the Soviet Union.

IN TRYING TO UNDERSTAND why it has been different with Bush, we arrive at what is truly new, and genuinely controversial, about the Bush Doctrine, especially in the form it takes in the Second Inaugural. It is not the universalism or the democratizing thrust that the President highlights in this speech and for which he has been so obtusely assailed; both of these, as we have just seen, are as old as the American Republic itself and both have served as lodestars for Democratic and Republican presidents alike. It is, rather, this President's repudiation of the longstanding "realist" policy of tolerating tyrants in the Middle East for the sake of stability, and his correlative effort to institute a new policy of "idealism" that conforms to the great liberating tradition of this Nation." Which—to the fury of the old foreign-policy establishment where the realist perspective still holds sway, and to the dismay of those conservatives who are skeptical about the conservative pedigree of the new policy and/or its viability—is exactly what Bush has done. As he reminds us in the Second Inaugural, because we have now extended this tradition to Afghanistan and Iraq, "tens of millions have achieved their freedom," and millions more, he predicts, will follow suit.

It is a daring prediction, but what gives it credibility is that the words Bush has spoken and the things the United States has already achieved under the aegis of his new policy have shaken the entire region to its core.

Listen to the testimony of the Lebanese dissident Walid Jumblatt who, only a few months earlier, had announced that "the killing of U.S. soldiers in Iraq is legitimate and obligatory," but who suddenly woke up to what those U.S. soldiers had all along been doing for the world in which he lived:

> It's strange for me to say it, but this process of change has
> started because of the American invasion of Iraq. I was cynical
> about Iraq. But when I saw the Iraqi people voting [in January
> 2005], 8 million of them, it was the start of a new Arab world.

Listen, too, to the Egyptian democratic activist Saad Eddin Ibrahim, who had also originally opposed the invasion of Iraq:

> Those [in the Middle East] who believe in democracy and civil
> society are finally actors [because the invasion of Iraq] has
> unfrozen the Middle East, just as Napoleon's 1798 expedition

did. Elections in Iraq force the theocrats and autocrats to put democracy on the agenda, even if only to fight against us. Look, neither Napoleon nor President Bush could impregnate the region with political change. But they were able to be midwives.

Free or relatively free elections have also been held for the first time elsewhere in the Middle East, and about them, the exiled Iranian commentator Amir Taheri had this to say:

Disappointed by the victory of Hamas in the Palestinian election and the strong showing of the Muslim Brotherhood in last year's polls in Egypt, some doubt the wisdom of pushing for elections in the Muslim world. . . . The holding of elections, however, is a clear admission that the principal basis for legitimacy is the will of the people as freely expressed through ballot boxes. In well-established democracies, this may sound trite; in Arab societies, it is a revolutionary idea.

Fouad Ajami, another commentator born and raised in the Middle East and a scholarly authority on its history, concurs in arguing that "while the ballot is not infallible," it has "broken the pact with Arab tyranny."

But the elections in the Palestinian Authority and in Egypt are not the only disappointments that have been suffered by supporters of the Bush Doctrine, and particularly those who are most passionate about its commitment to democratization. In some instances (as with Iran) Bush has moved at a slower pace than these fervent democratizers would wish and believe possible; in others (as with Syria and Saudi Arabia) there has been temporizing whose wisdom they question; and in still others (as with Egypt) there has been a failure to counter setbacks as forcefully as they think should be done. Some even accuse the President of thereby having betrayed the very assurances he makes when he addresses himself in the Second Inaugural directly to "the peoples of the world":

All who live in tyranny and hopelessness can know: the United States will not ignore your oppression, or excuse your oppressors. When you stand for liberty, we will stand with you. Democratic reformers facing repression, prison, or exile can know: America sees you for who you are, the future leaders of your free country.

Nevertheless, and for all the prudential considerations that have entered into the implementation of the new policy, the overriding truth is that, thanks to George W. Bush—and to George W. Bush alone—the Middle East has been "unfrozen" and that, whatever else may or may not happen, and no matter how many cautious hesitations and tactical detours or retreats may be dictated by prudential judgment, one thing is certain: so long as the Bush Doctrine remains in force, there will be no renewal of the old "pact with Arab tyranny."

Furthermore, the spillover effect of bringing our policy in the Middle East into line with "the great liberating tradition of this Nation" has begun to be felt in other regions as well. Thus, the nonviolent democratic Revolution that broke out in Georgia in 2003 and that inspired two others in the former Soviet Union (in Ukraine and then Kyrgyzstan), can be traced directly to the influence of the Bush Doctrine. We have this on the authority of the president of Georgia himself: "One thing I can tell you, Mr. President," he said to Bush on a visit to Washington, "your freedom agenda does, indeed, work. I mean, you can see it in Georgia." It is a development of this kind that lends weight to the universalist claim in the Second Inaugural that "we have lit . . . a fire in the minds of men," and that "one day this untamed fire of freedom will reach the darkest corners of our world."

TO BE SURE, the count is still far from in on this grand promise, even where the Middle East alone is concerned. Or perhaps I should say especially where the Middle East is concerned, since there are those who argue that the Muslim world lacks the necessary political, social, and economic preconditions for democratization. But this line of argument ignores or downplays or simply brushes aside the astonishing progress toward democratization that has already been made both in Afghanistan and Iraq. The same line of argument also runs afoul of the judgment of Bernard Lewis, the greatest contemporary authority on the region, who tells us that it is "demonstrably absurd in historical terms." In any case, Lewis adds, we have no choice: "Either we bring them freedom, or they destroy us."

But even if, as I believe, Lewis is right, there is still a long and rough road ahead. It took nearly forty years—with many reversals and missteps along the way—to defeat the Communists in World War III, and the chances are that defeating the Islamofascists in World War IV will—with its own reversals and missteps along the way—take as long or longer. It is even possible that we will lack the "patience" that Bush asks of us, and that we will desert the field before the Islamofascists and their terrorist shock troops are defeated by the tide of democratization that this President has unleashed.

Assuming, however, that we can steel ourselves to stay the course until victory is ours, it will be because in our American hearts and in our American bones we know that the President is right when he tells us in his Second Inaugural that our "vital interests and our deepest beliefs are now one," and that advancing the ideals that "created our Nation" is now "the urgent requirement of our nation's security, and the calling of our time."

The high nobility of this calling, and the incandescent words in which George W. Bush summons us to its service, are what convinces me that his Second Inaugural is one of the greatest speeches ever delivered by an American President.

(November 2006)

The Cultural Prerequisites
of Freedom and Prosperity

Lawrence E. Harrison

Mr. Harrison observes that America's universal ideal that "freedom and democracy are right and true for all people" has frequently clashed with the reality that some cultures are more hospitable than others to liberal ideals. Why have U.S. efforts to promote democracy succeeded in places like South Korea, Taiwan, and Spain but have generally failed in countries like Haiti, the Dominican Republic, and Nicaragua? He cites a number of reasons for such disparities but emphasizes the role of culture in the development of liberal institutions. Support for entrepreneurship, achievement, and merit, a belief in the importance of education—all are critical components in the building of democratic cultures. Democratization can succeed, he argues, but it must be viewed as a multi-faceted enterprise that involves reforms in both culture and policy. It should also be understood as a process that takes decades (rather than years) to mature.

The central conservative truth is that it is culture not politics that determines the success of a society. The central liberal truth is that politics can change a culture and save it from itself.

—Daniel Patrick Moynihan

CULTURAL VALUES, BELIEFS, AND ATTITUDES powerfully influence human behavior, and since those cultural attributes are widely shared in a society, they also powerfully influence the political, social, and economic evolution of the society, of the nation. Foreign and domestic policy makers, academics, and World Bank (among other) development specialists are reluctant to confront culture. But the failure to do so can be enormously costly for foreign policy, be it in the abortive imposition of democracy in Iraq or in efforts to accelerate the agonizingly slow pace of development in Africa, much of Latin America, and the Islamic world.

Virtually all the most successful countries in the world today, including those in Western Europe, North America, and East Asia, and Australia and New Zealand, practice democratic capitalism. All these countries have benefited from religions or ethical codes that nurture democratic politics or economic development, or both: Christianity, particularly the Protestant sects; Judaism; and Confucianism. The three share, among other values, the belief that people can influence their destinies and a related emphasis on the future; a high priority for education; the belief that work is good; and celebration of achievement and merit.

These values do not receive comparable emphasis in other religions/cultures, for example Islam and, to some extent, Catholicism and Orthodox Christianity. Such cultures tend more toward fatalism and focus on the present or the past. They attach lower priority to education—in the case of the Islamic countries, particularly for women; are ambivalent about the value of work and achievement; and often award status based on family, clan, or class rather than merit. The lag in the movement of these societies toward the goals of democratic governance, social justice, and prosperity enshrined in the UN Universal Declaration of Human Rights is in large measure the consequence of their progress-averse value systems.

MOYNIHAN'S OFT-REPEATED aphorism, which underscores the mutability of culture (it's not in the genes), challenges a concept that is at the root of the failure to confront culture: cultural relativism, an anthropological theory popular in the academic world that argues that one culture is not better or worse than any other—it is merely different. The theory may make people feel good, particularly if they live in poor, misgoverned, unjust countries—or egalitarian and righteous if they are First World anthropologists who adopt, in whole or in part, a poor, misgoverned, unjust country. But the theory is patently erroneous, at least when it comes to political, economic, and social progress.

Some cultures are prone to democratic politics, while others resist it. In his classic *Democracy in America*, Alexis de Tocqueville made an observation in the 1830s that is relevant today: "Mexico, as happily situated [geographically] as the Anglo-American Union, adopted these same laws but cannot get used to democratic government. So there must be some other reason, apart from geography and laws, which makes it possible for democracy to rule the United States." For Tocqueville, that reason is culture: "the habits of the heart . . . the different notions possessed by men, the various opinions current among them and the sum of ideas that shape mental habits."

Many economists would like to ignore culture. In his review of my 1992 book, *Who Prospers?*, William Easterly (the former World Bank economist and author of *The White Man's Burden)* wrote, "Maybe there is a lot to be said for the old-fashioned economist's view that people are the same everywhere and will respond to the right economic opportunities and incentives." Easterly's view ignores a salient fact: in multicultural countries where the economic opportunities and incentives are available to all, some ethnic or religious minorities often do much better than majority populations, as in the case of the Chinese minorities in Indonesia, Malaysia, the Philippines, and Thailand—and the United States. Why has the "Washington Consensus" prescription of free market economics, e.g., fiscal policy discipline, trade liberalization, openness to foreign investment, and privatization, worked well in India and poorly in Latin

America? Cultural factors are not the whole explanation, but surely they are relevant.

Alan Greenspan got it right when he said, after the collapse of the Russian economy in 1998–1999, "I used to assume that capitalism was human nature . . . it was not human nature at all, but culture."

If culture matters, then, what are the implications for a foreign policy a fundament of which is, "These values of freedom are right and true for every person, in every society"? In the long run, Francis Fukuyama argues in *The End of History*, all human societies will converge on the democratic-capitalist model because it has proven to be the most successful way of harnessing human nature to produce progress. I agree. But what about the short run? What are the chances of consolidating democracy—not just elections but also the full array of political rights and civil liberties—in Iraq, an Arab country with no experience with democracy, and with two conflict-prone Islamic sects, Sunni and Shia, and an ethno-linguistic group, the Kurds, seeking autonomy?

Arab countries in general rank very low in rankings of political rights and civil liberties according to studies conducted by independent groups like Freedom House. Democratic continuity is extremely rare in Islamic societies, Turkey coming closest to being an exception. According to the data I presented in *The Central Liberal Truth*, Islamic countries are low in trust, high in corruption, very low in female literacy, and high in fertility rates. These data strongly point to a fundamental cultural indisposition to democracy in that region. We should not be surprised by a headline in the July 1, 2006 issue of *The Economist*: "Democracy in the Arab World—Not Yet, Thanks. Recent hopes for the steady advance of democracy are being widely stifled."

GERMANY, JAPAN—AND IRAQ?

PRESIDENT BUSH'S frequent references to the democratization of Germany and Japan during the U.S. post-World War II occupation as models for Iraq are fundamentally flawed. Our military occupations of three countries in the Caribbean basin—Nicaragua, Haiti, and the Dominican Republic—in the early decades of the twentieth century may have far greater relevance.

At the end of World War II, Germany was a defeated, devastated country. But it had developed in the nineteenth and twentieth centuries a powerful economic, industrial, technological, and military capacity that enabled Hitler to seek domination of all of Europe and the Soviet Union as well. Germany led the world in literacy in 1900, and it had had an eleven-year experience (fragile to be sure) with democracy during the Weimar Republic (1919–1930). It was, moreover, a highly disciplined, substantially homogeneous society of the West, and profoundly influenced by Protestantism.

The circumstances were substantially the same in Japan after its unconditional surrender in 1945. Four years earlier, it had dominated much of east and southeast Asia, reflecting its highly developed economic, industrial, technological, and military capacity as well as a homogeneous, disciplined, educated, and skilled populace. Japan had eliminated male and female illiteracy in the first decades of the twentieth century.

It is true that Confucianism, a major influence on Japanese values and attitudes, nurtures authoritarian governance. But Confucianism, with its emphasis on education, achievement, and merit, can also nurture economic miracles that can in turn nurture democracy; witness the democratic transformations of South Korea, Taiwan, and Hong Kong, as well as Japan.

Its oil wealth notwithstanding, Iraq is clearly an underdeveloped country with a tiny industrial and technological base, a rudimentary infrastructure, and a largely uneducated, unskilled populace that is anything but unified. It is much closer to the condition of Nicaragua, Haiti, and the Dominican Republic in the early decades of the twentieth century when the United States intervened in them militarily in the interests of U.S. security, but also to promote democracy.

THE EARLY TWENTIETH-CENTURY INTERVENTIONS

IN A PERCEPTIVE ARTICLE in the March 2005 issue of *The Atlantic* magazine, the historian David Kennedy traces the ideological continuity in American foreign policy from Woodrow Wilson to George W. Bush anchored to the idea that "These values of freedom are right and true for every person, in every society." But Kennedy omits reference to Woodrow Wilson's involvement in the American military interventions in Nicaragua (1912–1933), initiated by Wilson's predecessor, William Howard Taft; Haiti (1915–1934); and the Dominican Republic (1916–1924), which combined elements of *Realpolitik* and what FDR's Latin America expert Sumner Welles would subsequently describe as "the role of the evangel . . . to reform . . . the conditions of life and government of the . . . sovereign republics of the American hemisphere."

Welles would go on to conclude, "All sense of proportion was lost."

The dubiousness, in the short run, of the credo "These values of freedom are right and true for every person, in every society" is underscored by the aftermath of those three Caribbean interventions in which Wilson played such a prominent role:

- The U.S. Marines occupied Nicaragua from 1912 to 1933 and attempted to install democratic institutions. But the occupation provoked an insurgency led by Augusto César Sandino, who became a hero throughout Latin America—a symbol of resistance to U.S. intervention. In step with Franklin Roosevelt's Good Neighbor policy, the Marines left in 1933. In 1936, National Guard commander General Anastasio Somoza García ousted the elected president, initiating a dictatorial dynasty that would last for forty-three years. A successful revolution led by the leftist Sandinistas—"children of Sandino"—forced Anastasio Somoza Debayle into exile in 1979, leading to another U.S. military intervention through aid to the Contras in the 1980s. Democratic continuity was established in the elections of 1990, but it is at best fragile and marred by extensive corruption.

- The military occupation of Haiti also provoked a militant reaction—the "Caco" insurgencies. The first insurgency was put down by the end of 1915. But a second insurgency, prompted in part by abuses of the U.S.-trained Haitian Gendarmerie, erupted late in 1918. The Gendarmerie was unable to contain it, but the First Marine Brigade succeeded in ending the uprising in mid-1920.

  My Lai and Abu Ghraib have antecedents: "Isolated instances of atrocities during the second Caco campaign led to Congressional investigations culminating in Senate hearings during 1921–22," Sumner Welles wrote.

  The Marines left Haiti in 1934. Haitian politics soon returned to the authoritarianism, exploitation, and corruption that had characterized most Haitian governments going back to independence in 1804. That continuity was symbolized by the Duvalier dynasty that abused the country from 1957 to 1986. The American military returned in 1994 to reinstall President Jean-Bertrand Aristide, and again in 2004 to escort him out and help try to make order out of chaos.

- The democratic institutions installed by the United States soon started to unravel after the Marines left the Dominican Republic in 1924, and Rafael Leonidas Trujillo, who had been groomed by the Marines to lead the National Guard, assumed dictatorial powers in 1930 that would last for more than three decades. Trujillo was assassinated in 1961, probably with the connivance of the CIA. Juan Bosch, who was elected president in December 1962, was ousted by the military in the fall of 1963. The succeeding military/civilian government fell apart in the revolution of April 1965, which precipitated another U.S. military intervention, this one motivated principally by concern, in retrospect exaggerated, that the revolution would lead to another Communist nation (a "second Cuba") in the Caribbean. The crisis passed and democratic continuity was established with the elections of 1966, in which Joaquín Balaguer, with clandestine help from the United States, defeated Bosch.

These three cases demonstrate how good intentions expressed through military force and money can be frustrated by cultures that are not congenial to democratic institutions. "These values of freedom are right and true for every person, in every society" ignores the lessons not only of these three cases but also of the more generalized problems of democratization in the Islamic world, Africa, and Latin America.

THE ALLIANCE FOR PROGRESS

ON MARCH 13, 1961, President John F. Kennedy announced the commitment of the United States to an Alliance for Progress with Latin America "to demonstrate to the entire world that man's unsatisfied aspiration for economic progress and social justice can best be achieved by free men and women working within a framework of democratic institutions." The expectation of the Alliance architects was that, within ten years, Latin America would be immunized from Communism and securely on the road to sustained, transforming economic growth and consolidation of democratic institutions.

The years following the assassination of Kennedy saw a revival of the traditional Latin American pattern of military coups—*golpes de estado* as they are called in Spanish. The administration of Lyndon Johnson made its peace with military governments in Latin America, the large majority of which were anti-Communist. The pattern of security interests trumping the democratic evangel has not been peculiar to Latin America. We have understandably been unwilling to promote democracy with zeal in key Mid-Eastern countries like Egypt and Saudi Arabia lest regimes favorable to U.S. interests be displaced by governments hostile to our interests.

The victory of Communist Salvador Allende in Chile in 1972 was viewed with alarm by the Nixon administration, and, while my sense is that the principal architect of the demise of Allende was Allende himself through his polarizing policies, at a minimum the overthrow of Allende by General Augusto Pinochet was welcomed by the U.S. government.

By the mid-1970s, much of Latin America was under right-wing military government, including Argentina, Brazil, and Chile. Cold War priorities again trumped the evangelical democratic current in our foreign policy. But with the election of Jimmy Carter in 1976, the priorities shifted, and democratization was restored to the prominence it enjoyed in the early years of the Alliance for Progress. Human rights became a high-priority goal of foreign policy. While the National Endowment for Democracy was formally established in 1983 during the Reagan administration, its roots go back to the Carter years.

A democratic wave swept over Latin America in the 1980s, starting in Argentina, where the military government's adventure in the Falkland Islands left it widely discredited and opened the path to the elections of 1983, won by Raúl Alfonsín. José Sarney was inaugurated in Brazil in 1985 as the first civilian president in twenty-one years. After losing a plebiscite in 1988, Pinochet agreed to leave power, and civilian government returned to Chile in 1990, with Patricio Aylwin as the first center-left *Concertación* president in a line that continues today with Chile's first female president, Michelle Bachelet. Also in 1990, the Sandinista government in Nicaragua was defeated decisively in elections by the democratic opposition led by Violeta de Chamorro.

The democratic wave finally reached Mexico in 2000 with Vicente Fox ending three-quarters of a century of the soft dictatorship of the Revolutionary Institutional Party.

But forty-five years after the Alliance for Progress was initiated, democracy is far from consolidated in Latin America. Hugo Chávez, elected president of Venezuela in 1998, has behaved increasingly like a traditional caudillo, albeit of the left. Presidents have been forced out of office in Ecuador and Bolivia, and term limits on presidencies have been extended in Argentina and Colombia. Corruption is rampant, except in Chile. Three recent presidents of Costa Rica, the "Switzerland of Latin America," are under indictment for corruption.

In 2006, forty-five years after the Alliance for Progress was inaugurated, democratic stability has eluded most of Latin America. Only Chile, Costa Rica, and Uruguay appear to be irreversibly democratic. Freedom House rates ten Latin American countries as "free," seven as "partly free," and one, Cuba, as "not free."

Disconcerting evidence of the weakness of the democratic vocation in Latin America is a conclusion of a recent United Nations survey of 19,000 people in eighteen countries: "A majority would choose a dictator over an elected leader if that provided economic benefits."

USAID DEMOCRACY PROGRAMS IN LATIN AMERICA

LIKE OTHER DEVELOPMENT assistance institutions, the U.S. Agency for International Development (USAID) has supported democratization programs throughout the Third World as well as in the former Communist societies in Eastern Europe and Asia. Such assistance is often provided through the international development institutes of the Democratic and Republican parties and business and labor groups.

Presumably, such programs would promote the values that make democracy work, including trust, association, and respect for the rule of law. But the experience suggests that ways must be found to strengthen these values *before*, or at least simultaneously with, the strengthening of democratic institutions.

In 2003, the Government Accountability Office (GAO), formerly the General Accounting Office, completed a study of USAID programs in support of democracy in six Latin American countries:

Guatemala, El Salvador, Nicaragua, Colombia, Peru, and Bolivia: $580 million of USAID funds were used between 1992 and 2002 to promote "the rule of law, transparent and accountable government institutions, respect for human rights, and free and fair elections" in these countries.

The GAO report notes some progress in the six countries but concludes that "helping to strengthen democracy can be a difficult and long-term challenge that requires sustained political support from key host country leaders. When this political support wavers, hard-won gains can be quickly lost."

Lurking behind the GAO findings is the message of Alexis de Tocqueville: *It is difficult (and probably impossible for outsiders) to build democracy without a critical mass of democrats.* Tocqueville's message obviously also applies to other parts of the world, including Afghanistan and Iraq.

Elections are the easiest component of democratization. External organizations with enough money and enough people may be able to assure that the people vote and that the vote is fairly counted. This was true of the elections in Haiti in December of 1990, won by Jean-Bertrand Aristide. But once the elections are over, making a society function democratically is vastly more difficult, above all if there is not a substantial democratic consensus and vocation among the people. Haiti is a case in point. Aristide was removed by the Haitian military in September of 1991 and restored to power through the intervention of U.S. military forces in 1994. Aristide's choice, René Preval, was elected president in 1995 and succeeded in 2001 by Aristide. But by then it had become apparent that Aristide was not a democrat. His overthrow by force in 2004 led to yet another chapter in Haiti's sad saga.

Of the six countries whose USAID democratization programs were evaluated by the GAO, only El Salvador seems to be making significant progress in the consolidation of democracy. El Salvador's political progress is probably linked to relative economic well-being, importantly the result of upwards of $2 billion in annual remittances from Salvadorans in the United States, "which dwarf every other industry in El Salvador," according to a PBS *Frontline* report in 2004. Here is a case where cultural change—and consolidation of democracy—may be driven by prosperity. (The annual remittances work out to about $350 per capita.)

THE NATIONAL ENDOWMENT FOR DEMOCRACY

THE NATIONAL ENDOWMENT FOR DEMOCRACY (NED) is an autonomous creation of the U.S. government which receives an annual congressional appropriation. It makes hundreds of grants around the world each year to support pro-democracy groups.

NED is far from the only institution, U.S. or otherwise, involved in democracy promotion. We have already referred to the extensive programs of USAID. The semi-autonomous Inter-American Foundation and Africa Development Foundation also include democracy promotion among its activities. The Department of Defense is engaged in democracy promotion activities in Iraq and Afghanistan. And myriad U.S. non-governmental organizations are also involved.

Moreover, many governments and private groups in Europe, Canada, and Japan attach high priority to democracy promotion among their development assistance activities. Finally, the international development institutions, above all the World Bank and UN Development Program, also dedicate substantial resources to democracy promotion.

Assessing the Endowment's impact is a task hugely complicated not only by the abundance of public and private entities promoting democracy around the world but above all by the dynamics of cultural, political, social, and economic forces within a country. But in reviewing NED's activities, Michael McFaul, director of Stanford University's Center on Democracy, Development and the Rule of Law, reaches a conclusion similar to that of the GAO with respect to USAID activities:

Especially where the goal is the eventual establishment of liberal democracy, democratization needs to be understood as a multi-faceted, potentially reversible process lasting decades rather than years.

The same may be said of cultural change.

But the role of the NED, and that of the several other U.S. government agencies pursuing similar goals, does raise a fundamental question in the context of this essay: If a culture to some meaningful degree compatible with democracy is a necessary precondition; if external pressures for democratization and externally financed programs to strengthen it are unlikely to work in the absence of internal leadership committed to democracy; and if non-democratic regimes are likely to reject programs that threaten their continuation in power, does it make sense for the U.S. to spend substantial sums of money promoting democracy?

I think it does, so long as we recognize that (1) the investment is for the long run; (2) that the effort is likely to be non-productive in the absence of internal leadership committed to democratization; (3) that we will run the risk of provoking hostility on the part of entrenched governments, institutions, and intellectual and religious leaders, particularly as the world's most powerful nation; and (4) that it may be difficult and perhaps impossible to attribute success and failure to our programs because there are so many other actors, domestic and international, on the stage. We must reconcile ourselves to a fact of life: at least in the short run, the priority of democratization is subject to subordination to political/security and possibly economic interests.

I believe that the programs of NED, USAID, and other public and private institutions would benefit if they analyzed the cultural obstacles to democratization and designed some of their interventions to promote cultural change that enhances democracy. My 2006 book, *The Central Liberal Truth* which derives its title from the second half of Moynihan's maxim, summarizes the findings of the Culture

Matters Research Project. This was a three-year effort involving some sixty-five experts around the world which I led at the Fletcher School, Tufts University. The final chapter, "Guidelines for Progressive Cultural Change," of *The Central Liberal Truth* covers a wide range of initiatives, for example, literacy programs, particularly for women; modifications to child-rearing practices and child-rearing education; education system reform; reform of religions aimed at promoting democratic capitalism; enlisting the media. USAID, NED, and others are already engaged in some relevant activities, but usually without appreciation of their potential for progressive cultural change.

U.S. ROLE IN SUCCESSFUL DEMOCRATIC TRANSITIONS

LET'S LOOK BRIEFLY at the U.S. role in the transition to democracy of Spain, South Korea, and Taiwan, in none of which was there any sustained democratic tradition worthy of the name and in all of which culture—Ibero-Catholic and Confucian—historically nurtured authoritarianism. In all three, a principal force for democratization was sustained high levels of economic growth that produced higher levels of education and a growing middle class, confirming Francis Fukuyama's belief that economic freedom and dynamism would inevitably produce pressure for political freedom.

In the case of Spain, the principal engine of economic growth was the opening up in the 1950s to foreign investment and tourism—and the opening up of Spain to the rest of Europe. (Up to that time, it was common to hear either "Europe ends at the Pyrenees" or "Africa starts at the Pyrenees.") By Franco's death in 1975, Spain was already far down the road of transformation: a rapidly growing middle class, significantly higher levels of education; more equitable distribution of income and opportunity; a military institution more imbued with the concept of civilian control; an increasingly pluralistic media; a Catholic hierarchy committed to democracy; and a Communist labor movement leaning away from Soviet influence toward the far more flexible "Eurocommunism." A rapid transition to democracy followed, ironically with Franco's hand-picked successor, King Juan Carlos, as guide.

The U.S. role in this Spanish "miracle" was largely indirect but not without impact. Because of its Cold War needs for military bases, the U.S. was the first Western democracy to breach the post-World War II quarantine of the pro-Axis Franco dictatorship. Close relationships between the American and Spanish military resulted, including training and orientation visits in the United States. The United States can claim part of the credit for the inculcation of the concept of civilian control of the military in the Spanish military establishment (albeit incomplete, as an attempted military coup in 1981 demonstrated).

Increasing numbers of Spaniards studied in the United States. Relations between Spanish and American businesses multiplied. And American (and European) tourists flocked to Spain. The Spaniards had an unprecedented opportunity to see what our country and our people were like. And the scars of 1898 notwithstanding (they were still present, as I discovered when I lectured in Madrid in 1994), many liked what they saw.

But the brilliant Spanish writer José Ortega y Gasset foresaw in 1910 what would be the principal external force behind Spain's transformation more than half a century later: "Spain is the problem, Europe the solution."

THE "MIRACLES" of South Korea and Taiwan closely resemble one another. The U.S. presence in both was motivated chiefly by security concerns: the threat from North Korea and China to South Korea, and the threat of Chinese invasion of Taiwan. Our military presence was substantial in both countries, and it persists in Korea to this day, albeit with resentment on the part of many Koreans.

Our stake in each country resulted not only in a strong U.S. military presence but also in high levels of economic assistance in the 1950s and 1960s. The U.S. influence on economic policy was thus substantial. As in Japan, highly effective land reform programs were implemented with U.S. assistance, making an important contribution both to democratization and the high rates of economic growth sustained by both countries.

Starting in the late 1950s, the U.S. encouraged economic policies heavily tilted toward the export promotion that has guided the economic miracles responsible for moving the two countries from the Third World to the First over a period of about forty years. We also facilitated the studies of large numbers of Korean and Taiwanese students in American universities, many of whom returned either to teach or take jobs in government. But at the heart of the miracles one finds Korean and Taiwanese entrepreneurship, emphasis on education and merit, achievement drive, discipline, and extraordinarily high savings rates characteristic of all societies influenced by "Confucianism," including China, Japan, Korea, Taiwan, Singapore, and Vietnam.

But Confucianism, so like the Protestant and Jewish ethics when it comes to economic achievement, tends to nurture authoritarian politics, importantly a reflection of the high priority it attaches to filial piety, both to the father and the father-figure ruler. In both South Korea and Taiwan, much of the economic miracle was achieved under military governments. The first civilian, Kim Young Sam, was elected in 1992.

Chiang Kai-Shek governed Taiwan in a highly authoritarian manner from 1949, when his Nationalists fled mainland China, until his death in 1975. His son, Chiang Ching-Kuo, paved the way for a gradual democratic opening. A ban on opposition parties was lifted in 1989. Legislative elections were held in 1991 and 1992, and the first direct election of the president took place in 1996. Four years later, the democratic transition appeared complete with the opposition Democratic Progressive Party's candidate Chen Shuibian the winner.

In summary, the principal contributions of the United States to the democratization of both countries were (1) the stabilization of the economies stretched thin by defense spending; (2) development assistance, including land reform and education; (3) extensive opportunities for young people to study in the U.S.; and (4) good economic policy advice.

CULTURE AND ECONOMIC DEVELOPMENT

AS WE REFLECT ON A HALF CENTURY of heavy emphasis on economic development, one question leaps to mind: Why did a few poor countries sustain transforming rates of economic growth while the vast majority, particularly those in Africa, Latin America, and the Islamic world, failed to do so? The evidence strongly suggests that some cultures promote the values and attitudes that encourage people to seize opportunities and respond to incentives—in a word, entrepreneurship—more than others.

The success stories include, in Asia, South Korea, Taiwan, Hong Kong, Singapore, and now China and India; in Europe, Ireland and Spain; and the Province of Quebec and Chile in the Western Hemisphere. No one factor can explain their success, although outward-looking economic policy played a role in all. The crucial role of good economic policy is apparent from two examples:

(1) From 1947 until 1991, India operated under statist/protectionist policies and experienced slow economic growth but with the subsequent opening up of the Indian economy, India has sustained 7 to 8 percent growth annually for more than a decade.

(2) South Korea moved from a country at roughly the same level of prosperity as a typical Latin American country in the 1950s to the First World fifty years later. During the same period, North Korea pursued socialism and is today among the poorest countries.

Yet India and South Korea were far from the only countries pursuing such policies, particularly after the Washington Consensus was announced in 1990. The Consensus policies were adopted by most Latin American countries, but in all except Chile, they failed to produce sustained high levels of growth. Obviously, a number of factors were in play, but I believe that one of the principal ones is the degree to which entrepreneurship is encouraged in a society. Ibero-Catholic culture has tended to suppress entrepreneurship except at the level of the elite, where, as Hernando De Soto observed in *The Other Path*, it often looks more like business-government collusion than entrepreneurship.

Chile enjoys an atypical tradition of entrepreneurship—Chileans provided considerable impetus to the Argentine economy as well as their own as far back as the late nineteenth century. While a part of the explanation for this anomaly lie in the uniqueness of Chile's history and geography, another part almost surely reflects the disproportionate Basque influence in Chile, the largest in Latin America.

Although several other non-cultural factors were also in play, for example, English-language proficiency in Hong Kong, Singapore, India, Ireland, and, ironically, Quebec; and proximity to Western Europe, culture also played a role either in terms of continuity or change. The East Asian economic "miracles," including the transformation of Japan in the late nineteenth/early twentieth century, were all facilitated by the continuity of Confucian/Chinese values, e.g., education, merit, discipline, achievement, and frugality, combined with a high priority for economic development (which is not characteristic of Confucianism). These same values lie behind the high levels of achievement of the overseas Chinese in such contrasting settings as Indonesia and the United States; the Japanese in Brazil and the United States; and Korean immigrants in the United States.

Sweeping cultural change occurred in Spain, importantly as a result of economic development. But in that country, as well as in Ireland and Quebec, the influence of the Catholic Church, particularly in education, declined sharply by the design of political leadership to the point where today the term "post-Catholic" is heard of all three. The value profiles of Spain and Ireland have converged with those of the Western European mainstream, while Quebec's value profile has ironically converged with Anglophone Canada's at the same time that the quest for sovereignty has surged.

Interestingly, Chile is the most Catholic country in the region—divorce was not legalized until 2004. But Chile, in an example of cultural continuity, has enjoyed (1) the atypical tradition of entrepreneurship noted above, and (2) atypically high levels of integrity in its public sector, apparent from its standing in Transparency International's Corruption Perceptions Index—tied with Japan at number 21 in 2005. (Costa Rica and El Salvador are the next Latin American countries on the listing, tied at number 51.)

"THESE VALUES OF FREEDOM are right and true for every person, in every society," is a viable foundation for U.S. foreign policy *if it is viewed as a long term goal.* In the short run, it must be applied very selectively to cases where the cultural, politico-social, and economic trends show signs of moving a society toward receptivity to democratization. One indispensable sign is the emergence of a critical mass of internal leadership committed to democratic transformation. *Except in rare cases, the transformation cannot be driven or managed from the outside, but it can be assisted.*

The cultural dimension of political, social, and economic development has largely been ignored, in part because it is difficult to quantify. But the evidence of the last half-century, during which a few countries have achieved democratic transformations and high levels of economic growth while most have failed to do so, strongly suggests a significant cultural component to development. Governments, development assistance institutions, universities, and research organizations need to develop capacity for cultural analysis.

The success of the advanced democracies—and above all the world's sole great power, the United States—in making democratic capitalism produce the greatest good for the greatest numbers; in advancing humankind's knowledge of the world around us and harnessing that knowledge for human progress; and in producing constructive, mutually rewarding, peaceful relations among nations will in the long run provide the most effective incentive for democratization and economic development to those nations that lag behind.

(December 2006/January 2007)

The Storks Are Landing

Daniel Johnson

Daniel Johnson offers a European perspective on America's role in the world and on its efforts to promote freedom and democracy abroad. Anti-American sentiment on the European continent, he argues, is more a consequence of a loss of faith in Europe itself than of anything the United States has done to provoke it. Indeed, as he points out, Europe has been a chief beneficiary of America's willingness to sacrifice blood and treasure to export its ideals. "Europe, the homeland of Western Civilization," he writes, "has mutated from a self-confident concert of powers, comfortable in the company of their bold and bumptious American ally, into a continent of querulous, carping prima donnas, quick to criticize anything and everything about the United States but unwilling to make sacrifices for anything beyond their own narrow horizons." Meanwhile, Europe itself is threatened internally by its own demographic crisis and the immigration of large numbers of Muslims determined to maintain their identity and to reject Western ideals. In his view, Europe indulges its anti-Americanism at its own peril.

THE QUESTION THAT ANIMATES THIS ESSAY is one that troubles not only Americans, but the friends of freedom and democracy everywhere. Why, when the rewards of liberty have been so amply demonstrated to the peoples of Europe over the course of the twentieth century, have they turned with such vehemence against the nation that rescued, restored, and is now again reinforcing those liberties?

Americans and Europeans may inhabit different continents, but they surely do not inhabit different planets. What is commonly called the West still identifies a coherent conception of what a civilization is, or at least ought to be. And in the defense of that civilization, Europeans are doomed by history and geography to occupy the front line. Just as Imperial and Nazi Germany dominated the mainland of Europe but never directly impinged on America, just as the Soviet Union occupied almost half of Europe but in the Western hemisphere never advanced beyond Cuba, so today the jihad poses a far more immediate threat to Europeans than to Americans. Yet the war on terror is viewed with a jaundiced eye from the opposite shore of the Atlantic: For many Europeans, it is America's war, not Europe's, if it is a war at all.

The most influential analysis of this transatlantic divergence has been that of Robert Kagan. As an American living in Brussels, he has been uniquely well placed to observe the workings of the European Union from within, while retaining the critical perspective of an outsider. His treatise *Of Paradise and Power* crystallized the rival perspectives into a series of neat contrasts: Kant versus Hobbes, peace versus war, multilateralism versus unilateralism, "soft" versus "hard" power. More recently, Kagan has filled out this aphoristic outline with *Dangerous Nation*, a closely argued and erudite narrative history of "America's place in the world" from the origins of the republic to the early twentieth century.

Kagan's argument in *Dangerous Nation* neatly dovetails with *Of Paradise and Power* by demonstrating that American readiness to undertake military intervention for humanitarian purposes was not an aberration, but "reflected Americans' view of themselves as the advance guard of civilization, leading the way against backward and barbaric nations and empires." America's martial idealism is rooted in the republic's founding vision of liberty under the law, was tested almost to destruction in the Civil War, and achieved full expression only in the global conflicts of the twentieth century. No other nation has so liberally sacrificed its blood and treasure for the sake of liberty; no other nation could have matched such sublime words with such substantial deeds. Humanity in general and Europe in particular owe the United States a debt of honor that is unprecedented in history.

It is a debt, however, that remains outstanding, at least as far as most of continental Europe is concerned. With notable exceptions among the "accession" countries of central and Eastern Europe, the only continental states to offer support to the United States in Iraq were Spain and Italy. In both cases, however, the right-of-center governments that took a pro-American line were punished by their electorates with eviction from office—notoriously, in the case of Spain, under the impact of the terrorist attack on Madrid. While it is true that the volume of anti-American rhetoric has recently been turned down in France, largely thanks to the Gaullist presidential candidate Nicolas Sarkozy, and even more so in Germany, thanks to the chancellor, Angela Merkel, the record of these two leading nations of the European Union inspires little confidence that a real change of heart is in the offing. For all intents and purposes, Europe has ceased to be a reliable ally of the United States. The continent has instead reverted to a complex patchwork of attitudes and allegiances such as existed before the Cold War, with the emergence of Islam as a major political factor serving to polarize opinion for and—mainly— against America.

IT IS ILLUMINATING TO COMPARE the reactions of Europeans to previous existential threats with the new threat posed by radical Islam. A fundamental difference between Europe's predicament today and those of the past is the absence of the unifying set of Judeo-Christian beliefs that have hitherto defined the civilization of the West. With St. Augustine of Hippo, Christians believed that the city of God was both stronger and incomparably more precious than the cities of men, and that pagan invasions were merely a means of divine chastisement: "Thus, in this universal catastrophe, the sufferings of Christians have tended to their moral improvement, because they viewed them with the eyes of faith."

The collapse of the Roman Empire in the West was not the end of civilization. On the contrary, the successive waves of barbarian peoples evoked a new kind of civilization, more robust than the ancient polis. Christendom, though never confined to Europe, was constitutive of Europe. When Europe began to deconstruct its Judeo-Christian inheritance, it tore up its roots. Europe forgot the truth about its own origins: that the salvation of Western civilization was made possible by the powers of endurance of Christianity, which in turn owed everything to the miraculous survival of the Jews. The progressive secularization of Europe, driven by what the Jewish scholar Joseph Weiler has called the ideology of "Christophobia," is exposing the civilization of the West to the very dangers against which the Judeo-Christian ethic of spiritual resilience in the face of temporal disaster had for so long protected it. Nor will the invocation of the Enlightenment as an alternative source of inspiration be sufficient. Like the Renaissance culture from which it emerged, the Enlightenment too was indebted to the Judeo-Christian traditions that had preserved the civilization of the West in its darkest hours. If the experience of the totalitarian pseudo-religions of the last century should have taught Europeans anything, it is that in the absence of the active defense of the Judeo-Christian conception of the moral integrity of the human person, the more utilitarian values of the Enlightenment alone cannot be relied upon to prevent a descent into unspeakable depravity.

In the medieval and early modern eras, Europe was able to resist external threats (primarily from Islam) by drawing on a warrior ethos, a conscious effort to cultivate martial virtues that lasted well into the twentieth century. That ethos is well summed up by G. K. Chesterton in his stirring poem *Lepanto*, which recalls the great clash of civilizations in 1571. The point of the poem is that while the crowned heads of Europe ignore the impending Turkish onslaught, the old spirit of chivalry that had animated the Crusades is not yet dead. "The last knight of Europe takes weapons from the wall." As the battle reaches its climax, Chesterton evokes the plight of the godforsaken Christian slaves who rowed the Turkish galleys: "Breaking of the hatches up and bursting of the holds,/Thronging of the thousands up that labor under sea/White for bliss and blind for sun and stunned for liberty." The point is that Europe, to survive, must connect the love of liberty with the courage to defend it.

Yet that courage is precisely what seems now to be lacking. The moral code under which Western Europe has operated since 1945 puts safety first, second, and third. Bravery is equated with bellicosity, chivalry with chauvinism, heroism with celebrity. Europe contemplates American feats of arms with barely disguised distaste. The bombing of Baghdad in 2003 was intended to induce shock and awe. It did so—but among the coalition's European allies no less than its enemies. In Germany the refrain was: "Haven't the Americans and British learned anything since Dresden?" The critics ignored the precision of the attack, which reduced civilian casualties to a minute fraction of those inflicted in comparable raids during the Second World War or even Vietnam. The objection was less to the destructiveness of the military technology than to the "gung-ho" enthusiasm of the men and women who fought what proved to be a tenacious and incredibly bloodthirsty foe. The mentality of the warrior, still considered worthy of respect in popular American culture, is regarded in Europe as undisguised fascism.

AND YET ALL AROUND US the generations that defeated the Kaiser and Hitler are quietly slipping away, their astonishing deeds disregarded, their decorations treated as mere curiosities. The heroes themselves refer to their exploits rarely, and when they do speak of them it is in a matter-of-fact way that belies the unimaginable circumstances in which they saved civilization from tearing itself apart. Day by day their obituaries record the lives of the survivors, a lost world of famous victories now fallen silent.

One of those who fought on the wrong side in both world wars was Ernst Jünger, who wrote a classic account of trench warfare—he was wounded fourteen times—*Storm of Steel.* Describing the last great German offensive in March 1918, he describes the mood on the eve of battle: "I sensed the weight of the hour, and I think everyone felt the individual in them dissolve, and fear depart." The dissolution of the individual in war is a fact that frightens Europeans today. For the soldier, however, it is precisely that selflessness that banishes fear. Nor does the collectivism of conflict necessarily mean that mercy is denied to individual enemies. He recalls an encounter with a wounded British officer in the same battle. Holding a pistol to his victim's head, Junger fully intended to shoot him. But: "With a plaintive sound, he reached into his pocket, not to pull out a weapon, but a photograph which he held up to me. I saw him on it, surrounded by numerous family, all standing on a terrace. It was a plea from another world. Later, I thought it was blind chance that I let him go and plunged onward. That one man of all often appeared in my dreams. I hope that meant he got to see his homeland again." It was not blind chance that made him spare his enemy, but the instinctive humanity that made Junger untypical of the Nazi-led Wehrmacht in which he nonetheless consented to serve two decades later. It is this magnanimity that still separates the West from the Islamic terrorists.

WHAT IS IT THAT has rendered Europeans so unwilling to rouse themselves in the defense of liberty that Americans so naturally regard as their vocation from God? Consider two examples of martial virtue that are almost commonplace in the United States. A former instructor at West Point, Colonel Blair Tiger, told me about the case of a female officer who had lost a leg in Iraq. Though invalided out of the Army, she missed active service, and after an interval she returned to West Point, eager to prove her fitness for duty. Colonel Tiger watched this woman attempt the extremely arduous assault course designed for able-bodied recruits. When she encountered a wall and was required to jump up to a high ledge, he fully expected her to give up. Not a bit of it: Nonchalantly unstrapping her artificial leg, she threw it up onto the ledge, and then with a supreme effort succeeded in hopping up. She climbed down on the other side, put her peg-leg back on, and carried on. Another example: When steel from the wreckage of the World Trade Center was melted down and used to construct the anti-terrorist assault ship USS *New York*, everyone involved—from steel workers at the foundry to the naval officers manning the warship—sensed the "spiritual" significance of this unique act of recycling.

It is not easy to imagine such scenes taking place in continental Europe. Most Europeans are no longer ready to lay down their lives for their fellow countrymen—or indeed for any other cause. True, we have been here before. In 1933, the year that the Nazis came to power, the Oxford Union, a debating society for the future British political elite, passed a notorious motion: "That this House would under no circumstances fight for its King and country." Hitler apparently took this as evidence that the British would never fight another war with Germany. Once the policy of appeasement was seen to have failed, however, the British did fight—unlike most of continental Europe. So, though we are undoubtedly living in a period of pacifism or even defeatism, the mood could change abruptly. This time, however, it is not true that—as a famous Victorian song had it—"We don't want to fight, but, by jingo if we do,/We've got the ships, we've got the men, we've got the money too." Europe has neither ships, nor men, nor money—or at least it is not prepared to spend money on war, least of all against Islamist terror.

Why not? The rot set in during the Cold War, which was the first time in history that Europe had not picked up the tab for its own military expenditure. For more than half a century, the United States has subsidized the "European pillar" of NATO. Indeed, NATO eventually came to be seen by cynical Europeans as a thinly disguised mechanism for extracting something for nothing from Uncle Sam. But now that the habits and virtues of martial fortitude that sustain peoples through long periods of conflict have decayed in Europe, it is apparent that the Americans had the better of the deal in the long run.

For those European states that possessed colonies, the Cold War coincided with decolonization. There can be no doubt that this process of imperial disenchantment lies at the heart of Europe's self-absorption. The loss was moral as much as territorial. Europe disencumbered itself of a burden, but the continent also lost much of its own *raison d'être*. The loss of empire mattered less in itself than as an abandonment of the peoples of Africa, Asia, Latin America, and Oceania to what often proved a hellish fate. Whereas the United States took on more responsibility for regions with which it had no historical connection, such as Southeast Asia, Europe abandoned its new creations with indecent haste. Most of the fifty million or more people who have died in wars since 1945 were the victims of Europe's abdication of its responsibility towards its former colonies. The damage inflicted on the European psyche by this loss of nerve, this failure of moral imagination, is incalculable.

IT WAS DURING THE SPANISH-AMERICAN WAR, the first humanitarian intervention by the newly self-confident United States, that Rudyard Kipling addressed one of his most politically incorrect poems to the American people. Today "The White Man's Burden" offends because of its racial overtones, but it is not really about race so much as responsibility. To the refrain "Take up the White Man's burden," the poet warns of the trials that lie ahead for Britain's American cousins: "The savage wars of peace/Fill full the mouth of Famine/And bid the sickness cease;/And when your goal is nearest/The end for others sought,/Watch Sloth and heathen Folly/Bring all your hopes to nought." Kipling evokes "The cry of hosts ye humour/(Ah, slowly!) toward the light:/'Why brought ye us from bondage,/

Our loved Egyptian night?'" Even more prophetic is another passage: "In patience to abide,/To veil the threat of terror/And check the show of pride. . . ." Kipling was well aware, too, that taking responsibility for another people invites the harshest of criticism at home: "Comes now, to search your manhood/Through all the thankless years,/Cold, edged with dear-bought wisdom,/The judgment of your peers!" President Bush could echo Kipling in the inner recesses of his heart—any less privately and he would never be forgiven—but of his European peers only Tony Blair would understand. The rest know little and care less about bringing freedom and democracy to benighted nations. What was once the European burden has become primarily an American one. And though Mr. Bush may wish that he had heeded Kipling's warning—"Nor call too loud on Freedom/To cloak your weariness"—his fault, if fault it be, is to have shown too great a zeal for liberty.

The European refusal, not only to assist in the overthrow of a tyrant but to give a fledgling democracy all possible assistance, is a measure of its decline. I once had an exchange with the German foreign minister Joschka Fischer at an embassy lunch about his country's failure to help Iraq to get back on its feet. Fischer protested too much, and his evident irritation betrayed the bad conscience of a postwar German who knew full well that his own people had not so long ago been rescued from a similarly desperate plight by the Yanks and the Brits.

The flight from faith and the ability to endure suffering; the revulsion from war and the virtues of the warrior; the abdication of responsibility that was once the concomitant of imperialism: These are all crucial factors in the transformation of the Old World's relationship with the New. Europe, the homeland of Western civilization, has mutated from a self-confident concert of powers, comfortable in the company of their bold and bumptious American ally, into a continent of querulous, carping prima donnas, quick to criticize anything and everything about the United States but unwilling to make sacrifices for anything beyond their own narrow horizons.

It is easy to forget how recent this transformation is. The revolutions of 1989 promised to bring "Eastern Europe"—a misnomer for lands that had once been wholly Western—back to life. The 1990s began with high hopes: the incubus of Communism banished, broken nations and lives healed, with both halves of the continent stimulated by the challenges ahead. Today, less than twenty years after this European epiphany, those hopes have turned to dust. The expansion of NATO and the EU cannot disguise the fact that these Cold War institutions have been hollowed out, and no longer embody any meaningful ideas. To adapt Dean Acheson's famous aphorism about Great Britain: The European Union has acquired an empire and lost its role.

WHAT IS GNAWING at the heart of Europe, rather, are two impending crises: demographic decline and the creeping Islamicization of the continent. These crises are inextricably intertwined. Whether or not he was the first to make the connection between demography and Islam, Mark Steyn has led the charge. *America Alone* makes the case that Europe faces a future of accelerating depopulation—unless mass immigration by rapidly reproducing Muslims fills the vacuum. His argument is that "Eutopia"—the pacific, welfare-cosseted, multicultural, green and pleasant land that the EU aspires to be—is on a collision course with "Eurabia"—the new generation of hostile, proselytizing, violent Muslim youths bent on turning their adoptive continent into a kind of Gaza strip writ large. For Steyn, a new Dark Ages beckons.

Yet the old adage "demography is destiny" is at best a half-truth. It was the pioneer of demography, the Reverend Thomas Malthus, who gained economics its reputation as the "dismal science"—and his prediction that industrialization would produce famine turned out to be wrong. By implication, Steyn acknowledges that the transformation of Europe into Eurabia is not inevitable—otherwise, why bother to polemicize against it? That America really is alone in possessing both the strength and the will to halt the march of Islamofascism, on the other hand, seems to me indisputable. So the question then becomes: How can Europe be mobilized to defend itself? Why, if the diagnosis is so obvious, is the remedy still so unpalatable?

ONE WAY OF LOOKING AT THIS is to identify those who are hindering the recognition of reality and then to tackle them. By far the most powerful obstacle remains the left, which still holds power in most European countries most of the time, and which usually sabotages any conservative leader who tries to break the consensus. Just as the left—with many honorable exceptions—advocated appeasement of Communism, so today they are busily accommodating themselves to the Islamists. In some cases, such as George Galloway's grotesque Respect Party in Britain, the alliance is overt. More often, though, it is more of a hard cop, soft cop routine. Aggressive secularization, expunging Christian morality from the law and excluding Christian voices from the public square, goes hand-in-hand with an informal acceptance of Sharia (Islamic law). The demonization of Israel represents a similar acceptance of Muslim anti-Semitism. A central tenet of the twenty-first-century left, too, is anti-Americanism. When in January, Tony Blair welcomed Condoleezza Rice to Downing Street, Peter Hain, a senior member of his cabinet, chose that day to denounce "the most right-wing American administration, if not ever, then in living memory" and declared that "the neocon mission has failed." These and similar sentiments have become an article of faith for most of the European left, and even for conservatives who wish to curry favor with the liberal media.

Yet the left is not monolithic, and there are dissenters. In Britain, Tony Blair is loathed by the left and now finds himself closer to neoconservatives on both sides of the Atlantic; yet the Euston Manifesto in 2006 brought together a group of left-wing intellectuals who support his stand against the jihad. They are joined by a growing number of writers and academics for whom the censorship, misogyny, and illiberalism associated with Islam are the main issues. Their voices are few but their cry of *j'accuse* hits home precisely because they cannot be dismissed as "right-wing." The betrayal of intellectual freedom by the European intelligentsia is nothing new. This time, however, the *trahison des clercs*, as Julien Benda called it, is even more blatantly against the interests of the intellectuals as a class than it was in the case of fascism or Communism. Islam, even in its more moderate form, has no place for the libertarian and libertine values that predominate in what they see as the decadent culture of the West. It is too late to do anything about the likes of Günter Grass and Gore Vidal, Noam Chomsky and Eric Hobsbawm. But younger intellectuals who do not wish to be re-educated in Mecca should be able to make common cause with conservatives on the issue of freedom of speech and the press.

The second major stumbling block for those who are serious about stopping Europe's slide into oriental despotism is the new Muslim establishment. Once marginal, Islam is now the fastest growing religion across Europe. Muslims now outnumber practicing Christians in many European cities, and mosques, schools, and other Islamic institutions have acquired power and influence to match. In many cases, however, they have simultaneously been radicalized. Funded largely by Saudi and other Middle Eastern oil money, Wahhabi influence is growing fast. The vast majority of British Muslims is not Middle Eastern in origin; most belong to the Sufi tradition, which is relatively tolerant. But many—probably most—British mosques are now under the control of community "leaders" who are radically opposed to the war on terror and whose loyalty to the Muslim "ummah" takes precedence over their allegiance to the Crown. It is hard to measure the precise extent of Wahhabi and other extremist influence, but a fairly reliable indicator is the attitude toward women: If they are excluded from the mosque, or segregated in a separate prayer room, it is likely to be hard-line. More than half of British mosques do in fact exclude women, and it is a similar story across Europe.

We can see the results of this radicalization wherever we look. To take a couple of examples: A terrorist suspect who had been subject to a "control order," restricting his movements and requiring him to report to the police every day, absconded and took sanctuary in his local mosque. The British authorities did not dare to arrest him in the mosque, so began protracted negotiations. While these were going on, the terror suspect was given a new passport and smuggled out of the country, probably to an al Qaeda training camp in Pakistan. Another case: An undercover reporter for the Channel Four documentary "Dispatches" filmed a radical preacher denouncing Western democracy before the council of a large mosque in Birmingham. Their only comment was: "When can you start?" The same program uncovered similar evidence of Wahhabi influence on the oldest and most prestigious mosque in Britain: the London Central Mosque in Regent's Park. Of course, it is not a one-way street: Finsbury Park Mosque, where the Islamofascist preacher Abu Hamza radicalized many young men who later became terrorists, is now under the control of moderates. One of them—a Somali refugee who had seen first hand the terrible consequences of Islamist sectarianism in his native country—told me exactly how the extremists had been systematically excluded. But these are rare exceptions.

What is to be done? Short of closing down at least half the mosques and subjecting the rest to close scrutiny, there is no simple solution. Moreover, such doctrinal invigilation would run contrary to the great tradition of religious toleration that goes back to Locke and Spinoza. Like Elizabeth I, we do not wish to make windows into men's souls; like the American Founding Fathers, we do not wish to impose religious tests for public office. Yet radical Islam is as much a political ideology as it is a religion, and Americans have never hesitated to ban members of subversive political parties, whether Nazi or Communist, from entering the country. Perhaps the best rule of thumb is to follow the money, which is the root of all evil, including Islamofascism. The criterion for toleration should be that identified by Pope Benedict XVI: that of reciprocity. No Islamic country that refuses to permit Christian, Jewish, or other non-Muslim worship should be allowed to flood the West with money to fund mosques that promote Wahhabi or other extremist forms of Islam. For example, the British obviously should not let Tablighi Jamaat, a missionary organization that intelligence experts suspect is a front for terrorism, to build the largest mosque in Europe in the East End of London, next to the site of the 2012 Olympic village. Saudi Arabia is not footing the bill purely for altruistic reasons, any more than the rest of the hundreds of billions of dollars that it has dispensed to promote Wahhabi Islam worldwide.

CONTROLLING THE CASH SUPPLY may not be sufficient, however. In the view of many, what is needed is an Islamic reformation. Quite apart from the fact that the Christian Reformation was followed by a century of wars of religion, the possibility of Islam actually undergoing such a reformation seems remote. As Pope Benedict has observed, the Koran cannot be reinterpreted because it is supposed to be not merely inspired by Allah, but his uncreated word, dictated to his prophet. As the Pope correctly argued in his Regensburg address, Allah, unlike the Judeo-Christian God, is not logocentric; to be a Muslim means to submit to the will of Allah, not presuming to understand the reason why. Sharia is divine and hence immutable; theocracy is preferred to democracy. The central role of jihad in Islam is not about to change, either. It is this doctrinal rigidity that causes many European Muslims to believe that America is attacking Islam, even though the truth is just the reverse. A religion that emerged in seventh-century Arabia must evolve and adapt if it is to be compatible with the Anglo-Saxon idea of liberty under man-made law on which the United States is based.

The best hope for Islam is not reformation but integration. While the theology of Islam is unlikely to be reformed any time soon, there is no reason why Muslims should not adapt to Europe, just as they have been adapting to various other cultures for fourteen centuries. This was the dream offered by the founder of London's Muslim College, Zaki Badawi, whose proudest boast was that he was a member of the Athenaeum, a club traditionally frequented by Anglican bishops. But when Badawi died last year aged eighty-four, his dream of a fully integrated British Islam was still unfulfilled. Instead, a very different dream inspires many young European Muslims: the dream of an Islamic republic under a restored caliphate. Combined with an aggrieved sense of victimhood and a perverted cult of martyrdom, this vision of a purer, universal faith becomes an unstable, volatile, and literally explosive fantasy. The young male fantasists who become Islamist jihadis attempt to live this dream. It has become Europe's nightmare.

In some places, that nightmare is already reality. Europe is now in the early stages of a *Kulturkampf,* a cultural confrontation between unreformed Islam and the modern nation-state. Europe has internalized the clash of civilizations.

There is potential here for a civil war that could tear Europe apart. Memories of Yugoslavia and Chechnya are still fresh. Yet the American example could still teach Europe how to assimilate its Muslims without conflict. Europe's multicultural model must be replaced by the melting pot, which inculcates American values while respecting religious differences.

THAT, OF COURSE, IS NOT ALL that Europe has to learn from America. Where the United States is democratic, the European Union is bureaucratic; where American capitalism is dynamic, European capitalism is static; where Americans are hopeful, convinced that they can solve all the problems of the world by their own efforts, Europeans are fatalistic, helplessly and hopelessly expecting the worst. Europe doesn't have to be that way. (Russia is another story.)

If it is to preserve its place as the heartland of Western civilization, Europe has no choice but to follow America's lead. America's hopes and fears are—or should be—Europe's, too. In Bosnia, Kosovo, and Afghanistan, this fact of life was eventually acknowledged, grudgingly and belatedly; not so in the case of Iraq. Europe is about to be tested again. When Iran supplies terrorists in Iraq to kill American or British troops, or when it menaces Israel with the threat of nuclear annihilation, Europe's reflexive response is to send diplomatic missions to discover what the Iranians "really" want. What, though, if the Iranian tyrant simply means what he says— defeat for the United States and destruction for Israel? Is Europe to stand idly by while Ahmadinejad carries on where Hitler left off? The most ignominious chapter in Europe's long history has been deliberately and indelibly imprinted on the collective memory of its peoples—but for what purpose, if not to prevent a repetition of the Nazi genocide? Iran, then, will be the supreme test of European resolve. If the pusillanimous politicians who strut the corridors of the chanceleries of Europe cannot bring themselves to act before it is too late— if, in short, they do not support President Bush when the moment comes to halt the Iranian Islamo-Nazis in their tracks—then Europeans will have proved themselves unworthy of their ancestors at Thermopylae and Marathon.

Five centuries ago, Martin Luther wrote in his treatise *Secular Authority*: "Frogs need storks." The Islamist storks are heading Europe's way—in fact, they have arrived. The question for Europeans is: Are they men or frogs? If they choose to heed Jacques Chirac rather than Tony Blair, then Europeans will get what they deserve.

(March 2007)

Liberty for Strangers
American Power and
the Predicament of the Arabs
Fouad Ajami

*In sending U.S. forces to overthrow Saddam Hussein and to estab-
lish democratic rule in Iraq, President Bush was acting on the basis
of principles of self-determination set down by his liberal predecessor
Woodrow Wilson. It is deeply ironic, then, as Fouad Ajami argues, that
today Western liberals, who otherwise applaud democratic reforms,
now regard democratization in the Middle East as nothing but a fool's
errand. Professor Ajami disputes the notion that people in Arab lands
are unprepared for democracy and unworthy of any sacrifice on the
part of Westerners to bring it about. The campaign for democracy in
that region remains vital both to our interests and ideals because (as
he writes)," As long as the Middle East remains a place where freedom
does not flourish, it will remain a place for stagnation, resentment, and
violence for export."*

IN THE SCHEME of American diplomatic history in the Arab-Islamic
lands, the advocacy of freedom in those domains is of recent vintage.
If a date is to be given for the birth of this diplomacy, it would have
to be President George W. Bush's speech to the National Endowment
for Democracy on November 6, 2003. There was fervor in that speech,
and belief. Indeed, there was a startling *mea culpa* for decades of

American diplomacy: "Sixty years of Western nations excusing and accommodating the lack of freedom in the Middle East did nothing to make us safe—because in the long run, stability cannot be purchased at the expense of liberty. As long as the Middle East remains a place where freedom does not flourish, it will remain a place for stagnation, resentment, and violence for export. And with the spread of weapons that can bring catastrophic harm to our country, and to our friends it would be reckless to accept the status quo."

It was not naive idealism that had given birth to the diplomacy of freedom. November 2003 had been a time of crisis. Seven months after the destruction of his regime, Saddam Hussein was still on the loose, and the hunt for weapons of mass destruction had run aground. The war, and its sacrifices, had to be given a new rationale, and the emphasis on liberty would come to animate American diplomacy. In his second Inaugural Address, President Bush would proclaim the new doctrine yet again: "All who live in tyranny and hopelessness can know: The United States will not ignore your oppression or excuse your oppressors. When you stand for liberty, we will stand with you." It wasn't unfettered, this new diplomatic drive, but it had blunt messages for the rulers in Tehran and Damascus, and there was a shot across the bow, it should be recalled, intended for the regimes in Riyadh and Cairo. Indeed, the rulers in these two pivotal realms were being put on notice that the traditional deference to their ways no longer obtains.

No one was under any illusions about the kind of work it would take to open up the entrenched regimes in Saudi Arabia and Egypt. Few if any believed that there were brigades of liberals in these places waiting for a sign from the Americans. It was known in the way such things are known that the opponents of these regimes were themselves often at odds with American values. Arabia was *terra incognita*, a realm virtually sealed to outsiders. America had been on the ground there for well over six decades, but its access to the culture, and to the wellsprings of the society, was limited in the

extreme. It was known that the opponents of the House of Saud—
the opponents who mattered—were not liberal Western-educated
types, but zealous ultra-Wahhabis who had begun agitating against
the realm in the aftermath of the Gulf War of 1990–1991, on the
grounds that the rulers had "defiled" the realm by opening the
Arabian Peninsula-the land of the Prophet and the revelation—to
a vast American military presence. The House of Saud may have
"winked" at religious fundamentalism, it may have given fodder
to the religious extremists, protected itself by tolerating, perhaps
encouraging, a malignant anti-Americanism. But these rulers had
worked out the terms of an accommodation with the custodians of
American power. No one in the circles that mattered in American
foreign policy genuinely believed that Arabia would sprout a "liberal" alternative to the rulers. It had been the prudent thing to let
well enough alone.

EGYPT UNDER ITS AGING AUTOCRAT, Hosni Mubarak, presented
a different challenge. Where Arabia lived off its wealth, the Egyptian
regime received American largesse, at the same time as it let play in
its land a dark anti-Americanism. This was the homeland of al Qaeda's influential Cairene, Ayman al-Zawahiri. It was from the ranks of
Egypt's Islamists that al Qaeda's most embittered and vengeful activists had emerged. In Egypt's prisons and torture chambers, it could
be said, the seeds had been sown for trouble to come. A meandering
road led from the assassination of Anwar al-Sadat, in October of
1981, to the Islamist terrors a generation later. Young Islamists had
come of age, but the military regime had thwarted their schemes.
Zawahiri himself had been picked up in the dragnet that followed
Sadat's assassination; he had been imprisoned and tortured, he had
taken to the road, vowing to return to a land cleansed by an Islamic
rebellion. It was he who had made that essential distinction between
the "near enemy" (the regime at home) and the "distant enemy" (the
United States). The man in the saddle in Cairo was at once an "ally"

in the war on the terror, and a source of so much of the resentment that gave rise to the terror.

Sly and cunning, Mubarak had reduced the political life of Egypt to a standoff between his security apparatus on one side, and a dark, incoherent Islamist movement on the other. He had bullied the middle class, brazenly imprisoned the few secular intellectuals who had dared question his monopoly over the life of the land. He had been brutal with a noted academic at the American University of Cairo, the sociologist Saad Eddin Ibrahim—a man who held American citizenship at that. He had him dispatched to prison, as he did the political oppositionist Ayman Nour, who was given a five-year prison sentence.

American power was at a loss as to what to do with Mubarak. He was bribed and cajoled, he was given access to President Bush, he also had a portion of Egypt's aid withheld on one occasion. The Secretary of State traveled to his domain with an appeal to Egypt's liberal tradition, a call on the country to remember a rich and vibrant political life before the time of the military autocracy. In a widely covered speech at the American University of Cairo, on June 20, 2005, Secretary Rice called up the best of Egypt's national memory, its pride in its struggle for social and cultural emancipation. "Throughout its history, Egypt has always led this region through moments of greatest decision. In the nineteenth century, it was the reform-minded dynasty of Muhammad Ali that distinguished Egypt from the Ottoman Empire and began to transform it into the region's first modern nation. In the early twentieth century, it was the forward-looking Wafd Party that rose in the aftermath of the First World War and established Cairo as the heart of the 'Arab Awakening.' And just three decades ago, it was Anwar Sadat who showed the way forward in the entire Middle East."

This detour into history, this open appeal to the country's better nature, played out against the background of a dismal political standoff. The regime's goons were terrorizing peaceful demonstrators in Cairo's streets, the ruler was showing every sign that he had in mind a dynastic succession for his son. And the Secretary of State would make an allusion to all that: "Now the Egyptian Government must put its faith in its own people. We are all concerned for the future of Egypt's reforms when peaceful supporters of democracy—men and women—are not free from violence. The day must come when the rule of law replaces emergency decrees—and when the independent judiciary replaces arbitrary justice."

A vigorous debate was raging in the inner circles of the Bush administration about Hosni Mubarak. The Secretary of State had brought it out into the open. An uneasy battle lay ahead. The Americans could never arrive at the right policy toward this most populous of Arab states. The cunning military autocrat knew the game: He stalled then fell back on Egypt's instinctive suspicion of outside domination. The opponents of the regime were a checkered lot: Islamists at odds with Western values, liberal secularists given to pan-Arabism and to a reflexive anti-Americanism. The place invited American intervention—and balked at it at the same time. Pharaoh held out to the Pax Americana the familiar bargain: He would keep the peace (and the terrorists) at home, but his ways would have to be accepted. There were limits to America's power, and this military ruler tested them. He took America's coin, but went his own way. He opposed America in Iraq and second-guessed it on Israeli-Palestinian matters. He belittled the cause of liberty, he was the cop on the beat giving every indication that things would not change in his realm. Mubarak waited out America's moment of confidence, and he took the carnage in Iraq as a vindication of his own belief that the Arab lands—his above all—were ill equipped for freedom.

THE LANDSCAPE OF ARAB POLITICS was known—problematic rulers and, often, worse oppositionists. In the wings, there lurked the Islamists, and the rulers were shrewd enough to remind us of the terrible choice that lay before American power. But the force of the history that America unleashed by upending the regime of Saddam Hussein had its claims. In Iraq, a virulent insurgency warred with the new politics, but there can be no denying the hopes stirred by two national elections and a constitutional referendum held in that country. On the eve of Iraq's first national election, the mayor of Baghdad caught the mood of the time, and the hopes pinned on Iraq. "The rulers of the region are nervous, the people of the region are envious," the man said before the new order in Iraq would descend into a war for its very life.

And there was Lebanon, a country modern and "hip" enough to be familiar to the American sensibility. In the aftermath of that terrible crime that took the life of the former Prime Minister Rafiq Hariri on February 14, 2005, the Lebanese appeared to retrieve their land from Syrian tyranny. A dominion of three decades was abandoned, as Syrian forces raced across the border. It was fear of American power that had brought down the edifice of Syrian hegemony in Lebanon. The Pax Americana hadn't always been enamored of Lebanon. Its Western outlook and its Christian communities notwithstanding, American diplomacy over the preceding quarter-century had all but consigned Lebanon to Syrian rule. The Lebanese were warring sects, and America was understandably reluctant to be drawn into their affairs. (Beirut was a city of tactics, the clear-eyed George Shultz once observed of the place as he came to master its ways in the 1980s.) But here, too, there could be felt the breeze of freedom. American power would claim Lebanon's escape from Syrian captivity as one of the principal achievements of its campaign for liberty.

"We entreat America to do all it can to ensure that a small number of authoritarian rulers will not control the future of more than 300 million Arabs, more than half of whom are not yet 20 years old," a large group of Arab and Muslim activists and thinkers, more than one hundred in all, wrote in an open letter addressed to President Bush in late 2006. "Freedom and democracy are the only way to rebuild a world where violence is replaced by peaceful public debate and participation, and despair is replaced by hope, tolerance and dignity." Herein lay the dilemma of Arab liberalism: It has not been

www.encounterbooks.com

Please add me to your mailing list.

Name

Company

Address

City, State, Zip

E-mail

Book Title

ENCOUNTER BOOKS

900 Broadway

New York, New York 10003-1239

able to win on the ground, it could not hold its own against the auto-crats, or against the weight and the power of Islamist radicalism for that matter. It was left with petitioning a great, foreign power—a power, it has to be conceded, many of these same petitioners did not fully trust or support.

This was in keeping with an old history: In the inter-war years, a fragile Arab liberalism unable to contend with the appeal of col-lectivist doctrines of every stripe, and with the power of the estab-lished order of tribes and monarchs, wrote a self-serving history that explained away its weakness as a result of its betrayal at the hands of the Pax Britannica—and of the French. It was said by the embattled liberals that they would have had a chance had it not been for the Arab debacle in Palestine, and for the diplomacy in that struggle, and around it, that had tarnished British reputation, and by extension, the standing of the liberal project itself. In this argument, Britain and France, the two mandatory powers, had not sent the best of them-selves into the region. It was not the heirs of Voltaire who had come to Greater Syria but the colonial Troupes du Levant and the Senega-lese and Moroccan troops who put down popular rebellions. Britain had not come at the peak of its confidence to enlighten and educate (as had been the case in India a century earlier). It was a war-weary power that had made its appearance in Arab lands in the aftermath of the First World War, keen to achieve hegemony on the cheap, and to rule with air power and deals with tribes and dynasties.

By the late 1930s and early 1940s, Fascist and Nazi ideas would blow through Arab lands, seducing the young, offering them a false dream of grandeur and national power. Liberalism, it could be said, was never in contention. The rise of avowedly illiberal forces and the drumbeats of the Muslim Brotherhood were heralds of things to come. What the late Anglo-Arab historian Albert Hourani dubbed "Arabic thought in the liberal age" would come to grief. Henceforth the Arab political world would pass to monarchs and officers and religious guides. The liberals would be reduced to the squabbles of frustrated intellectuals. An "anti-imperialist" ideology, easy and smug, the diet of political men without power, would seal their fate.

IT IS AS TELLING A TESTIMONY as any on the weakness of Arab liberalism that it was only the American war in Iraq that had given this political current a new lease on life. There was supreme irony in all that. Iraq had always been seen by other Arabs as the "wildest" and most checkered of Arab lands—a frontier country at the intersection of Arabia, Turkey, and Iran, a country with a tradition of political violence. True, Arabic letters and poetry had owed a great deal to the Iraqis. But it would be fair to say—though Iraqis would contest this—that Baghdad lagged behind Beirut, Cairo, and Damascus, in the age of the "Arab awakening." But it was in Baghdad in 2003–2005 that a new Arab experiment was unfolding—the drafting of a constitution, and a referendum that sustained it, two national elections held in the shadow of a terrifying violence. Those elections were, vicariously, pan-Arab affairs. Men and women were not voting in Egypt, or in Syria or in the Arabian Peninsula. These Iraqi voters holding up to the cameras their index fingers dipped in purple ink were partaking of a tradition that dictatorship and revolutions had pushed aside in Arab life.

This new history was of course playing out under American tutelage. It was George W. Bush, and the war he waged, that had given birth to this new political experiment. The Arab critics of this Iraqi project—self-styled secular intellectuals in Amman, Cairo, and in the Arab diasporas in North America and Western Europe—could dismiss this Iraqi experiment as a cover for American hegemony. And they would find it easy to see in the results of the elections—the triumph of the big Kurdish, Shia, and Sunni Arab electoral slates—a victory for sectarianism and for the politics of identity.

"And how many military divisions does Arab liberalism have?" George W. Bush surely had reason to ask in 2006. He had bet on freedom in Iraq and in Lebanon, and he had put the Palestinians before a historic choice: They could have statehood or the ways of terror and violence. By late 2006, these three Arab realms were reeling. In Iraq, the bloodshed had all but obliterated the political life and the elections. In Lebanon, the "Cedar Revolution" which had looked so promising a year earlier had yielded to a great standoff, and Hezbollah had run away with the politics of the Shia—the country's largest community. President Bush had not bet heavily on the Palestinians—he had been wise to correct for Bill Clinton's obsession with the fight between Israel and the Palestinians. The Palestinians were to hold an election in early 2006, and they were bound to falter.

What exactly was the difference between the masked men of Hamas and the masked men of Fatah's Aqsa Martyrs' Brigade? This was the inheritance that Yasser Arafat left behind. Arafat's successor, Mahmoud Abbas, was a fairly decent man; he had promised order, he had tried to pull Palestinian society back from the violence that had been raging in it since the "Second Intifada" that had erupted in the year 2000. But Palestinian society had been greatly damaged; authority in it issued from a good throwing arm and from the rifle. Faced with a choice between Fatah's reign of plunder and corruption and Hamas's politics of zeal, the religious diehards of Hamas had prevailed.

This new political way had not yet had its run. But we judge quickly today, and the critics of this diplomacy of freedom were anxious to proclaim its demise. We had shaken up that world only to reap a whirlwind, it was said. We had bet on freedom, but the Arabs did not have it in their DNA; we had come from afar only to discover that those who would wager on the reform of the Arab condition would be plowing the sea. It was into this climate of opinion that the Iraq Study Group headed by James Baker and Lee Hamilton released its reading of that war, and of the stakes in it.

A generation earlier, we had known Baker as a supreme fixer. He had had a tin ear for the great struggle that played out on his watch as steward of American foreign policy—the demise of the Soviet Union, the breakup of Yugoslavia, the end of the post-World

War II international order. More to the point, he and Bush Senior had stood idly by as Saddam Hussein put down, with great cruelty, the Shia and Kurdish rebellions that President Bush called for in the course of the first Gulf War. Baker had returned unrepentant; by his reckoning he was to be our guide into the old bazaar in the region. He carried with him an old branch for the old order: In his and his Study Group's report, there would be little if any talk of freedom and reform. This was the "Rolodex diplomacy" of years past. We were to "engage" the rogues (Syria and Iran) and to defer to the chameleons at the helm of the Sunni Arab regimes. Those Sunni Arab regimes had been the source of our malady: It was their disaffected children, pitiless younger warriors, who had brought death and destruction onto American soil on 9/11 and set America on the road to Kabul and Baghdad. They were now to be forgiven.

FOR ALL OF THE POWER that America would deploy in Arab lands, and for all the exhortations, America could not want freedom for the Arabs more than they wanted it themselves. The foreign power that had come with this new gospel of freedom could not force its own civic ideas on a stubborn Arab world or uphold these ideas in the face of a dark Sunni-Shia feud that made its re-appearance in the region. (It had been fought out in the 1980s, in the time of the civil war between Ayatollah Ruhollah Khomeini's millennial revolution and the Sunni order of states in the Arab world.) More problematic still, America would remain oddly susceptible to the representations made to it by the Sunni Arab regimes about the menace of radical Shi'ism. Sunni fundamentalists had brought death and ruin onto American soil on 9/11, we had battled a primitive Sunni movement in Afghanistan, and the Sunni Arabs had taken up arms against America's new order in Iraq. Still, we now would be warned that our troubles can be laid at the doorstep of a resurgent Shi'ism.

True, a big ideological and security challenge had risen in the region, a new Persian challenge from the east. We had Moqtada al-Sadr in Iraq, and Hezbollah's Hassan Nasrallah in Lebanon, turbaned

Shia clerics, armed sayyids. They were crude and avowed enemies of the American presence in Arab lands. They were outsiders who had risen to sudden power. And they were, to the Sunni rulers, a perfect solution. Here was an opportunity to spook the foreign power, to enlist it in defense of sectarian privileges and phobias. If these two clerics were the harvest of democracy in Iraq and Lebanon, the autocratic order would have an easier time returning to its old accommodation with the Pax Americana.

There wasn't much that the old Arab order of states could—or would—do for America in Iraq. Indeed, the very order America sought to midwife in Iraq was anathema to the Arab regimes. Whether we willed it or not, we were empowering the Shia (and the Kurds). For well over a millennium, Arab Shi'ism had not governed. There was a brief reign of a Shia dynasty (of Persianate origins at that) in Baghdad in the middle years of the tenth century; it had been followed by a Sunni restoration, and an unbroken history of Sunni ascendancy. The whole weight of that order of power was arrayed against the success of Iraq—the weight of the rulers, and of the oppositionists alike, the religious warrants given the deeds of terror in Iraq, the Arab satellite television channels granting air and cover for the "resistance" and its brutalities. The one gift these neighboring Arab states could grant to Iraq and to their American steward was the one they would never give: They could stem the tide of the jihadists from their midst making their way to Iraq. But Iraq today is what Afghanistan was a generation earlier: a dumping ground for a fierce breed of pitiless younger men who could not reconcile themselves to the prevailing order in Arab lands.

A shrewd merchant in Kuwait who knows the ways of the region saw sure failure stalking this new attempt to go back to the autocracies. It is too late for that, he observed to me. That order's power is hollow, and the Americans themselves, he said, had emptied it of its power. "Look at the trial of Saddam Hussein, it played out on television, gavel to gavel. Ordinary Arabs could see for themselves that the rulers are not deities. Think of Hosni Mubarak expressing horror that

Saddam Hussein, once a fellow ruler, was sent to the gallows. This entire order rests on $60 or $100 or $150 per barrel of oil; it had been bailed out before by high oil prices. If and when these prices should tumble, the fragility of the edifice of Arab power will be there for all to see." This man of Kuwait, unsentimental about his world, had a fair reading of the Arab malady. For there is today a kind of Arab absence from history, and the lands of the Arab world seem like a battleground between Pax Americana and Iran. In the shadows, the Arab political class in the "moderate" states warns of the danger of an ascendant Iran. In their fashion, these Arabs would like nothing more than an American military campaign that would lay waste to Iran's nuclear ambitions and put an end to this new Persian menace. But we can be sure that when the dust of that strike settled, the Arabs would be out and about maligning America's imperial ways. Americans are strangers in that world. What order we provide, what liberties we secure, will always be the offerings of a foreign power: They are to be taken without an open acknowledgement of the debt owed the giver.

IT COULDN'T HAVE BEEN EASY WORK, this new project of repairing Arab lands. America did not know that world with the intimacy and detail it should have. We had given protection to the Cedar Revolution, and soon all the fratricide at the heart of Lebanon's tormented history came to the fore. "The feeling of devotion to the little native country does not exist among Lebanese officials and everyone of them is always ready, according to a well-known local expression, to set his country on fire to light his cigarette," one Joseph Couget, a French diplomat who knew Lebanon, observed in a memorable verdict decades ago. In no time, the Lebanese—with help from the Syrian tyranny next door, and from the Iranians further afield—would be back to the feuds of their history.

Lebanon's Shia community now faced a great choice: home and hearth and Lebanonism on one side, subservience to Syria and Iran on the other. Doubtless, untold numbers of Shiites wanted fidelity to home, and order and normalcy. But there were men with guns, and Iranian money, and an ability to frighten others into submission. There was Syria, temporarily chastened but gaining in confidence as its rulers realized that they had been spared. And there was a long history of Shia disinheritance, and that history would be skillfully used by Hezbollah leaders who had risen from the lowest rungs of a class-ridden society and were determined to fight for their newly acquired power. There was no denying the nobility of rescuing Lebanon from its long Syrian captivity. But we judge quicker today, and it was easy to despair of Lebanon, to write it off as a utopian campaign gone awry.

It was Iraq, of course, that would determine the fate of this new American push into Arab lands. It had been there where the statues were toppled, where a constitutional document was drafted, and where the Pax Americana had proclaimed its new faith in the ability of the Arabs to break with tyranny. And it would be there, three or four years into this undertaking, where the scales would tip against the cause of freedom. It would be fair to concede that Iraq in 2006 was not the envy of Arabs in other lands, or a source of worry to the Arab rulers that their populations would want for themselves what was playing out in Iraq. To be sure, the Arabs themselves were feeding Iraq's flames, but what mattered was the confidence of Iraq's neighbors that liberty had been shown to be a reckless undertaking. The dominant order in the region had nothing of its own to offer, it had bet that the foreign power would weary of its work, and that the terrible habits of centuries—the weight of retrogression, the sectarianism, the absence of civic traditions—would carry the day. Iraqis could plead that they needed more time or that it was yet too early to write off this project in their country, but the belief that this was a land inhospitable to freedom had acquired new respectability. No one had the perfect "strongman" to put forward for Iraq, but authoritarianism was being held out as the answer to the bloodshed.

In truth, the American regency has had a difficult time coming to terms with the Shia coalition leading the fractious government in Iraq. The Shia political leaders, Prime Minister Nuri al-Maliki included, hailed from the modest social classes of their community. Their knowledge of the American political system was limited in the extreme, and they had not had anywhere near the traffic and experience with America possessed by their counterparts in the neighboring Arab capitals. The feeling had taken hold among them that America had all but written them off to accommodate the Sunni Arabs within Iraq and beyond. These men were strangers to America's ways. They had their history. They were told that the "realists" had returned to positions of great power in American diplomacy. What they knew of these realists, of James Baker, and of Brent Scowcroft, what they remembered, was that these men were in the inner sanctum of power, back in 1991, when their rebellion, and that of the Kurds, were put down with great heartlessness and indifference. That kind of "realism" is viewed with dread by a people who tell history in metaphors of justice and betrayal.

HISTORICAL ANALOGIES are always flawed. But one offers itself as a precursor for Bush's diplomacy of freedom: the noble but doomed struggle on the part of Woodrow Wilson to sell his country on his peace program in the aftermath of the Treaty of Versailles. The Realist tradition does not think much of that chapter of American diplomacy. But generations of Arabs and Muslims always retained the memory that point twelve of Wilson's Fourteen Points urged that the former subjects of the Ottoman Empire be given "an opportunity for an autonomous development." The gospel preached by Wilson was the one great message of reform that would continue to resonate in Arab lands. We know what became of the Wilsonian program at home: A crusading president was rebuffed and frustrated by Henry Cabot Lodge of Massachusetts and William Borah of Idaho and a Senate that would turn back Wilson's program. Wilson had not been a match for the detractors and skeptics at home. Wilson scholars and sympathizers remind us that the American people were not prepared, in 1920, for the world leadership—and the burdens—

that Wilson offered them. But they further add that history would vindicate him—the apocalypse that would come two decades later, then the search for collective security that had been Wilson's cause all along.

It will be said that the analogy with Wilson and Wilsonianism overreaches, that Bush had stumbled upon his diplomacy of freedom in the course of the Iraq war, and that he was merely in search of a rationale for a war that had turned deadlier and more difficult than the early expectations had prophesied for it. But Wilsonianism, too, had been an improvised affair, and the man who had let loose its passions had not been fully prepared for what was to come. "When I gave utterance to those words"—that all nations had the right to self-determination—"I said them without the knowledge that nationalities existed, which are coming to us day after day." Wilson's secretary of state, Robert Lansing, thought it calamitous that Wilson had taken up so dangerous a course. "It will raise hopes which can never be realized. It will, I fear, cost thousands of lives. In the end it is bound to be discredited, to be called a dream of an idealist who failed to realize the danger until it was too late to check those who attempt the principle in force."

If Bush had come to the Middle East unprepared, so had Wilson. Point Twelve—the whole interest in the former domains of the Ottoman empire—was owed to Wilson's close friendship with a Princeton classmate, Cleveland Hoadley Dodge, a devout Presbyterian, an industrialist, and a philanthropist deeply involved in the affairs of the Near East, and in the flagship of the Presbyterian missionaries, the Syrian Protestant College (later renamed the American University of Beirut). His grandfather had been one of the five benefactors who incorporated the college. Dodge himself was to prove a steady supporter of Wilson—he was the largest contributor to his two presidential campaigns; he would be one of a handful of people who would set up an annuity for Wilson when his presidency came to an end. Dodge was driven by a passion for the Armenians, and for the Near East. "The industrialist," writes historian Joseph

Grabill, "sought a strategic American presence in the lands of the Ottoman empire." It had been Dodge who gave sustenance to the idea of an American mandate in Armenia in 1919–20; the effort was stillborn, along with the rest of Wilson's program. But the Wilsonian idea would endure, and the American missionary spirit would leave its indelible mark on the early phase of Arab nationalism.

Wilson had given birth to an intellectual and political inheritance way beyond his modest expectations for it. Henry Kissinger, one of America's most influential and brilliant practitioners and theorists of Realpolitik, gave the Wilsonian inheritance its due in remarks that bode well for Bush's diplomacy of freedom: "The League of Nations failed to take hold in America because the country was not ready for so global a role. Nevertheless, Wilson's intellectual victory proved more seminal than any political triumph could have been. For, whenever America has faced the task of constructing a new world order, it has returned in one way or another to Woodrow Wilson's precepts. . . . In Wilsonianism was incarnate the central drama of America on the world stage: America's ideology has, in a sense, been revolutionary, while domestically Americans have considered themselves satisfied with the status-quo."

WE CANNOT KNOW with confidence what will become of this campaign to make the Arab-Muslim world less deadly both for itself and the outside world. On November 7, three years to the day after President Bush's speech to the National Endowment for Democracy, the voters handed control of Congress to a new majority that had shown scant interest in the affairs, and the redemption, of the peoples of the Arab and Muslim world. They were not exactly "isolationists," the men and women who now controlled that branch of government. But there was a hesitant "Come Home, America" that could be discerned through their utterances. They did not tell us outright that they did not believe that democracy can travel to Arab lands (political correctness would preclude that sort of candor, for it had always been conservatism that argued that culture determines political outcomes) but this much, too, could be inferred about them. For them, it was enough that the diplomacy of freedom had been George W. Bush's program, and they wanted nothing to do with it.

Setting political correctness aside, a foreign policy luminary of the Democratic Party, Senator Joseph Biden of Delaware, in a television interview of December 10, 2006, on the ABC news program "This Week," put the matter in stark terms. He had seen President Bush, he said, and the President had reiterated his belief in the universal appeal of liberty. "He has this wholesome but naive view that Westerners' notions of liberty are easily transported to that area of the world." Biden of course knew better. He had warned the President that democracy is "more than elections," that Grand Ayatollah Ali Sistani's view of liberty differed from "our view of liberty. . . I think the President thinks there's a Thomas Jefferson or Madison behind every sand dune waiting to jump up. And there are none."

For a self-professed liberal internationalist, this was remarkable language and imagery. There had always been in liberal internationalism a measure of coyness about the ability of liberty to slip borders, and to put down roots in cultures beyond the West. Cold War liberalism had committed travesties of its own in Third World settings. But the American idea of liberty had always had a strain of optimism and redemptionism. Three years into the Iraq war, and the Bush stewardship, liberalism now spoke in entirely different terms. There were no liberals in those forbidding "sand dunes." It was the smart and safe thing now to say that these Arab-Islamic domains were lands of despotism; Joseph Biden was simply giving voice to this "knowingness."

Without a long view of history, without an explanation that would situate the Iraq war in the broader struggle with Islamic terror, Iraq had turned into a great American disappointment. There crept into the commentaries a harsh and dismissive tone about Iraq and Iraqis in particular: Iraq's people were now warring tribes, cruel and vindictive, and given to timeless feuds. Liberalism in its American variety had historically been based on the belief in Liberty's ability to skip borders; this principle, often violated in practice, had nonetheless been the central difference between the European and American strands of liberalism. American liberalism now left it to a conservative American president to uphold liberty's appeal and the possibility of its spread in Arab-Islamic lands.

IN TRUTH, THE ARGUMENT that liberty springs from within and cannot be given distant peoples is more tendentious than meets the eye. In the sweep of modern history, the fortunes of liberty were in no small measure dependent on the structure of power in the order of states. The will of the dominant power—or powers—in the world mattered greatly to the fortunes of democratic governance and to its appeal. Samuel Huntington and Robert Dahl, two of democracy's principal theorists in our time, have made this point with telling detail. In fifteen of the twenty-nine democratic countries in 1970, democratic regimes were midwifed by foreign rule, or had come into being right after independence from foreign occupation. In the ebb and flow of liberty, power always mattered, and liberty always needed the protection of the ascendant states in the international order. "The Americans are coming," it was widely believed in the Arab world in 2002–03, and the Islamists and the dictators scurried for cover in the aftermath of the destruction of the Taliban regime. There is in those lands a keen eye for the seriousness, and the will, of outside powers. The greater confidence shown by the enemies of liberty three or four years later derived from a reading by these forces that the tide had turned within America itself.

At its core, the Bush program rested on a linkage between their freedom out there in Islamic lands, and our security here at home. After Kabul, we had swept into Baghdad, because Kabul had not sufficed. We were guided, subliminally, by a correct reading of that arc of trouble in the Arab-Islamic world. It was from the Arab world that our troubles had come. But with the mounting costs of the Iraq war, more and more Americans came to see this linkage between American security and the repair of the Arab world as imposing intolerable burdens; they now wished to release themselves from the vigilance of 9/11, and the wars fought in the aftermath of that terrible day. In a democratic system, the majority will have its way. And this cause of freedom in distant lands would now contend with a curious mix of obstacles: the difficult soil of Arab-Islamic political culture, and the conviction in liberal American opinion that it was a fool's errand to take liberty to strangers.

(April 2007)

The Ebb and Flow of Global Liberty

Michael Novak

There is no way around it: America's efforts to promote freedom in the world and protect her own security from Islamic extremism are ultimately dependent on success in Iraq. Michael Novak makes a compelling argument that retreat and failure in Iraq will be taken by our adversaries as a sign that the West is a "weak horse" that is vulnerable to further attack. Though the struggle in Iraq has been difficult, it has had some important successes, most notably in the series of peaceful elections through which the Iraqi people have selected leaders and adopted a constitution. There are clear signs, he says, that democracy is in retreat around the world and that the enemies of democracy would like nothing better than to see President Bush's democracy project discredited in Iraq. A defeat in Iraq would only accelerate this trend, while a victory might turn events in a democratic direction.

AS WE REVIEW THESE ESSAYS on the meaning of liberty, three large questions loom before us. First, what can we learn from the ironies and the tragedies of the Coalition effort to build democracy in Iraq? Next, has the extension of the Lincolnian policy that President Bush announced in his Second Inaugural now proved to be impractical— the positive promotion around the entire world of "government of the people, by the people, for the people"? Third, what today is the greatest threat to liberty?

1. THE CASE OF IRAQ

TOPPLING THE REGIME of Saddam Hussein in Baghdad in 2003 required only three swift weeks of rapid armored attacks by Coalition forces. Soon afterwards, immense new difficulties welled up from the deep. Lawlessness broke out, and a combination of al Qaeda and Baathist raiding parties caused as much mayhem as they could. Armed bands turned, as if by traditional habit, to violence, slaughter, revenge, and bitter rivalry. In addition, the Iraqi inexperience in many preconditions of actual democracy—inexperience in democratic compromise, a loyal opposition, habits of cooperation, accommodation, and peaceable ways—made the transition from democratic voting to democratic governance uncertain, even stormy.

Ironically, each Coalition success was met by a new form of opposition. When Saddam's army was defeated, the foreign-fed insurgency erupted. When the insurgency was no longer able to meet the U.S. Army or Marines head-to-head in the field, even at platoon-size, suicide bombers and roadside devices multiplied. When these began to subside, al Qaeda leader Abu Musab al-Zarqawi tried to ignite a spiral of mutual retaliation between Shiites and Sunni, bombing the most sacred mosques and prompting massacres of 200 Shia here, 150 Sunni there. His aim seemed to be less to enable one faction to dominate the other than to destroy any hope of democratic governance under a rule of law.

Some political experts had long argued that not all peoples are "ready" for democracy. Outsiders, they said, may be able to lead peoples unprepared for democracy into the structures of democracy, but if the latter choose to relapse into mutual destruction, that is their own dreadful choice. In any case, the volatile situation in Iraq in 2005 and 2006 raised many questions about the practicality of promoting democracy in regions with little experience with free institutions. As Christopher Orlet tartly observed in late 2006, "There is more to liberal democracy than voting one day and slitting your neighbor's throat the next. There is an independent judiciary, human and civil rights, freedom of press, speech, etc., tolerance and pluralism, majority rule with rights for minorities, and most importantly there is basic local governance and security. Democracy has a long way to go in Iraq."

Protecting freedom for all citizens—the firm foundation of democracy—is a long-term project, Tocqueville reminds us:

> There is nothing more prolific in marvels than the art of being free; but there is nothing harder than the apprenticeship of freedom.... Freedom ... is ordinarily born in the midst of storms, it is established painfully among civil discords, and only when it is old can one know its benefits.

Democracy is also a fragile project. Where there is no respect for the rule of law, violence can easily overwhelm it—until all parties recognize that the "war of all against all" means in the end their own death, too. Only then, perhaps, does the search for government by mutual consent arise, through mutual respect for the natural rights of all, and the search together for institutions to secure those rights.

2. MEASURING FAILURES AND SUCCESSES

LET US COUNT UP, FIRST, THE SUCCESSES of the democratic project in Iraq. Although many predicted in advance that the following actions could not be successfully completed, the people of Iraq were able, even under threat of death, to vote in very large numbers both for a temporary government tasked with preparing a constitution for public ratification; and then, in due course, and in even larger numbers, for that ratification. The constitution, as adopted, was not perfect in the eyes of outside observers, yet it was difficult for anyone to point to a better one among the Muslim peoples in the Middle East. The new constitution at least opened up the path toward greater experimentation in protecting the free exercise of religion by Muslims and non-Muslims alike. Unhappily, later outbreaks of intimidation against non-Muslim believers caused far too many of the latter to lose heart and flee for their own safety. That failure clouded the larger success.

The new constitution also sharpened the differentiation between the separate roles of the clergy and the state authorities. The constitution as drafted tried to strike a balance between continuing in some form the historical influence of Islam upon the state, while recognizing the two-sided principle that the Mosque does not control the state, nor the state the Mosque. Further experience is now suggesting favorable adjustments to that balance.

Finally, the constitution, perhaps properly, did not settle the longstanding conflicting claims of the three main ethno-religious groupings of the Iraqi nation—the majority Shia who predominate in the South, the minority Sunni who predominate to the West, and the Kurds of the North. The beginnings of power sharing were put in place, representing all three groups, and are no doubt subject to adjustment as experience will point out. The foreshadowing of some future sort of federalism is also discernible in the constitution, with many details left to be worked out.

One of the most grievous problems faced by any scheme of federalism, however, is the fact that the capital city, Baghdad, is heavily intermixed with Shia and Sunni, and many large cities (Kirkuk, Mosul, and others) also have mixed populations. The infliction of constant harassment of one group upon the other, often through rival death squads employing torture and mutilation, seems aimed at inducing mass migration, or perhaps simply submission to the terror masters. One has not yet seen the formation of whole rival armies in the field, truly engaged in open civil war. But visible enough are homicidal bombings in marketplaces, nightly kidnappings, murders, assassinations, and other mayhem that almost all find weightily depressing, and some find unendurable.

The regime of organized torture and arbitrary violence practiced for decades by Saddam Hussein and his sons has left behind bitter memories that few who are not Sunni would like to relive. Meanwhile, current fears of violence reduce many in urban centers to uncertainty and fear, to a degree not long sustainable. In October of last year, Richard Nadler, writing on *National Review Online*, offered a helpful comparison of the death toll under Saddam to the number of Iraqis tragically killed by insurgents after the fall of his regime: "Scholars of civilian mortality place the daily Saddam-era toll of regime-caused deaths between 75 and 125 citizens per day— roughly double-to-triple the average post-war mortality reported by the body-counters. The death toll of the past two months, unusually bloody in four of Iraq's 14 provinces, has matched this range."

Thus, one condition of the success of the democratic project in Iraq had not been met by the end of 2006: the enforcement of security and good order in urban centers, beginning with the capital. This task is rendered harder by the steady invasion of hostile terrorists across the Iranian and Syrian borders. These, in turn, join up with indigenous insurgents to prevent democracy. For these foes of democracy, no outrage is too terrible. They have stooped to the heavy bombing of ancient, singularly beautiful, and long-cherished mosques, rejoiced in the assassination of clergymen and worshipers on holy days, and invented other schemes of barbaric murder. Democracy at all times is easier to destroy than to build. Even a few determined men can undermine it.

Nonetheless, even in the year of al Qaeda mayhem, Iraqis reported belief that their lives will be better in the near future. A June 2006 survey conducted by the International Republican Institute revealed that nearly half of Iraqis believed the future of Iraq would be better in a year; one-quarter believed conditions would be the same—neither worse nor better. While 41 percent believed Iraq is heading in the right direction, only 13 percent believed withdrawal of Coalition forces from Iraq should be the top priority to turn the country in the right direction. Eighty percent of Iraqis were confident in the Iraqi government announced by Prime Minister Nouri Al-Maliki. More recent polls by the BBC/ABC report that, after the ruthless violence of the insurgency during 2006, only 43 percent of Iraqis thought their lives were better than before the war.

MANY HIGHLY ACTIVE POLITICAL PARTIES are at work among Iraqis. More than 4,000 non-governmental associations, both international and indigenous, have sprung into life. Since June 2003, these associations have built and repaired 830 schools and 337 roads, launched 298 health-related initiatives, and improved 292 electric utility centers. Further, they are helping to advance civic education, women's advocacy, anti-corruption, and human rights. But much of this work had been disrupted by the end of 2006.

Nonetheless, many informal institutions and active associations of civil society have blossomed in Iraq, as they had not during the Saddam decades. All these developments are crucial parts of "the democracy project." The law of association, Tocqueville wrote, is the first law of democracy.

In democratic countries the science of association is the mother science; the progress of all the others depends on the progress of that one. Among the laws that rule human societies there is one that seems more precise and clearer than all the others. In order that men remain civilized or become so, the art of associating must be developed and perfected among them.

What renders a people a people, and not merely a mob, is a rich, thick, and variegated social life prior to and more basic than the institutions of the state.

New automobiles and other large-scale consumer goods have begun to be visible in stores, on the streets and in homes. Under Saddam, independent media were banned. And yet in free Iraq in only three years there were fifty-four TV stations, 114 commercial radio stations, and 268 independent print organs. Although California is a state comparable to Iraq in area and population, the media choices of "multi-cultural Angelos" are less varied than those in Baghdad today.

Furthermore, by overcoming immense obstacles, the successful trial of Saddam Hussein and the bringing down of a guilty verdict, the court system of Iraq struck the clearest possible signal of equal justice before the law, for the mighty as well as the lowly. No doubt the conduct of the trial was ragged (not least because of the antics of the defense), and no doubt immense fortitude was required on the part of all the principals in the case—defense attorneys and prosecutors, as well as the judges. Yet all seemed to have done their duty.

Few if any countries in that region possess comparable systems of law under which former heads of state might face indictment and trial. The symbolic tremors of the trial of Saddam Hussein are likely to be felt in the region for many decades to come. This is the point recently made by Fouad Ajami:

> Iraq and the struggle for a decent polity in it had been America's way of trying to extirpate these Arab troubles. The American project in Iraq has been unimaginably difficult, its heartbreak a grim daily affair. But the impulse that gave rise to the war was shrewd and justified.

He adds:

> American power and the very force of what had played out in the Arab-Islamic lands in recent years have rendered the old order hollow, mocked its claims to primacy and coherence. The moment our soldiers flushed Saddam Hussein from his filthy spider hole, we had put on display the farce and swindle of Arab authority.

Since the fall Saddam's regime in 2003, the accomplishments of the democracy project in Iraq are many and admirable. Nonetheless, the steady stream of terrorist attacks within Iraq (paid for and fomented by her nearest neighbors Iran and Syria) may in the end prevent Iraq's democratic project from being brought to success. Domestic insurgents with their armed militias and willingness to engage in extreme acts of violence may succeed in engulfing the entire country in a civil war.

To measure the dimensions of the tragedy that would ensue from open civil war would not be easy—but all of this humiliating and bloody unwinding of a once-noble experiment in democracy would be broadcast worldwide by Al Jazeera television. Following such a debacle, who in the future would want to ally themselves with the United States in a project to build democracy? Where would we find allies willing to take risks on behalf of democracy and liberty?

The circumstances in Iraq, of course, are in many ways unique. On its eastern border lies its ancient antagonist, Iran, in our time the great paymaster and clearinghouse of worldwide terrorism. Wealthy, ambitious, and worked up to a high pitch of fervor, Iran is motivated by a far more bloody vision than the building of democracy. This vision has two parts. Its more moderate focus is simply the re-establishment of the ancient Caliphate, that is, unified Muslim rule from Spain and Portugal on both sides of the Mediterranean, and on through the whole Middle East toward the great centers of Muslim population in Indonesia, Bangladesh, India, and the Philippines. Included in the dream of this Caliphate are the subjugation, humiliation, and taxation of all who refuse to submit to Allah, in the secondary status known as *dhimmitude*.

In the more extreme version of this vision, some Iranians already imagine the subjugation of all Europe to Islam through migration, greater fertility, and skillful intimidation. One hears some speak of subduing nations as far to the north as the Netherlands, Denmark, and Sweden by the year 2030. In a yet more extreme vision, the president of Iran has publicly ranted about a nuclear holocaust that would

116

vaporize Israel, and also precipitate the end of the world, which will lead to the return of the long-absent Mahdi, sword aflame.

3. THE END OF THE DEMOCRACY PROJECT?

THE SALIENT FACT in Iraq since March 2003 is that its people did not reject democracy, but rather acted often heroically in braving threats of violence against them by streaming openly to their voting stations. And not just once, but three times during three long years of danger-fraught elections, ever greater numbers turned out to vote. This one stubborn fact suggests that a substantial majority of Iraqi adults prefer to live under the rule of law, under limited government, and under governments formed and altered by their own consent. This one fact does not prove that this majority has the skills, the leadership, the organization, and even the ferocity to fight for the durability of what they have begun.

Alas, the record shows that a small determined band of some 12,000 insurgents can bring about enough destruction and disruption to intimidate the rest of the population, thus suffocating democratic institutions before they can establish themselves. This band of intimidators does not even have to create chaos, only the appearance of chaos. They carefully stage their most demonstrative accounts where the security-conscious Western media can film it, and then circulate the scenes around the world. Few of us know that in actuality, there were on average 112 cars a day torched across France in 2006. Very few were seen on American television (certainly not every day, not even once a month). The point is not to contrast the degree of violence in Iraq with that in France, but to note the difference in the press's fascination with the two events..

Suppose, however, that at some point armies of Shia and Sunni, numbering in the thousands begin to engage in open warfare in the major cities of Iraq, routing and killing hundreds or thousands of civilians in the process. In that case, we would all agree that precision demands speaking of civil war in Iraq. Does such an outbreak of civil war mean that the American policy of "democracy promotion" has failed in Iraq—and, by extension, *cannot* work, where there are other strong anti-democratic forces willing to be ruthless?

As critics of the Iraq strategy such as Thomas Carothers write, Iraq is not the only place in which democracy seems to be going backwards. We may even be witnessing a kind of "democracy demotion":

> After two decades of the steady expansion of democracy-
> building programs around the world, a growing number of
> governments are starting to crack down on such activities
> within their borders. Some ... have begun to publicly denounce
> western democracy assistance as illegitimate political
> meddling.

Vladimir Putin has quietly and steadily built up a new police state in Russia, an autocracy of the pre-Communist model, but with all the nefarious cruelties mastered by the Soviet KGB during the seventy-four-year life of the Soviet Union after 1917. In Hungary, too, on October 23, 2006, evoking awful scenes from the worst Soviet years, police ringed the main city square and bloodily cudgeled unsuspecting crowds. The police had been ordered to prevent any large gathering on the fiftieth anniversary of the Hungarian Uprising of 1956. This looks very much like the return of the old order in those countries. Not everywhere, but in a few key places, the anti-democratic thugs are back.

The ruthless assassination of a cabinet minister in the new democracy of Lebanon on November 21, 2006, flashed yet another signal in the gathering global darkness. Add to these Hugo Chávez, the latest *caudillo* in a long Latin American tradition, boastfully deploying Venezuela's oil wealth to grow steadily in his capacity to intimidate, subvert, and inflame weak neighboring governments. As the world learned in 1933, the mere fact of an electoral process does not prevent a dictator from entering upon and exercising power.

One senses again that the lights are going out one by one around the world, just as many sensed in 1914 and later in 1939.

Further, at least four nuclear powers are today exercising brazen moves to divert, distract, dissipate, and eventually undermine American military power—China, Russia, Iran, and North Korea. All have become adversaries of democracy and the democratic project inspired by the United States and its allies.

Recent books, such as Bruce Bawer's *While Europe Slept*, Tony Blankley's *The West's Last Chance*, and Claire Berlinski's sensitive and frightening report, *Menace in Europe*, recount from personal experiences the intensity, irrationality, and ferocity of the loathing for America among Europe's high-brow elites. One really does sense that during the next thirty years the United States might be "standing alone," as Mark Steyn puts it in the title of his recently published book, *America Alone*. As a new threat gathers in the Moslem world, the United States will be left to confront it without the allies in Europe on which it depended in the twentieth-century conflicts with fascism and communism.

If, then, one weighs the world balance of power at the present moment, at least on the face of things, "democracy promotion" is not in the ascendancy. It seems, rather, that this fragile growth is more vulnerable every day to attacks from a growing number of adversaries. Are we in fact near the beginning of a new era in history that will mark the gradual decline of democracy and liberty?

INDEED, PRECISELY AT THIS POINT another grievously wounding criticism has been launched against President Bush's "democracy promotion." Even he cannot cling to this principle in all cases; he himself has had to turn a blind eye toward non-democratic regimes such as Egypt, Saudi Arabia, Putin's Russia, and many others. But it is to be doubted that Bush has a lesser sense of the irony and tragedy of history, or less respect for the art of the possible, than his perfectionist critics. In Bush's mind, the principle of democracy promotion is not to be taken as a one-size-fits all, all-nations-at-once, operational handbook. It is to be understood as a long-term goal, a lodestar, a point on the compass, towards which we can look to find our way through the present storm. As President Bush said in his Second Inaugural:

> The great objective of ending tyranny is the concentrated work of generations. The difficulty of the task is no excuse for avoiding it. . . . Some have questioned the global appeal of liberty—though at this time in history, four decades defined by the swiftest advance of freedom ever seen, is an odd time for doubt. . . . We do not accept the existence of permanent tyranny because we do not accept the possibility of permanent slavery.

Mr. Bush throughout his political career in Texas and as President has many times shown his respect for doing what is possible, pressing forward steadily but taking detours and setbacks as circumstances necessitate. Democracy is a morally worthy goal, but it is neither an inflexible moral imperative nor a procrustean bed. To temporize, to take a step back in order to go forward at a more propitious time, to push as much as the traffic will bear—this was precisely Abraham Lincoln's tactic in regard to slavery. (At one point, Lincoln even turned Southern states against Stephen Douglas on the ground that if States could "choose" slavery they could also choose not to heed the Fugitive Slave Act. In this way he used a seemingly pro-slavery argument for his long-term goal of defeating slavery.)

Democracy requires a politics of compromise—a step forward from which nobody gains everything he wants, but everybody gains at least a little—and a politics respectful of irony, tragedy, the law of unintended consequences, and the principle that the perfect is the enemy of the good. Democracy is the opposite of utopian. Democracy is a humble and imperfect system, driven by a morality of the imperfect and the partial, but one that presses onward toward the good. Sometimes that is only the best good achievable at this time, a rather chastened sense of the good, but a noble and mature one.

Thus, it was not naive idealism that led Bush to call attention to this fundamental principle of American policy. As Fouad Ajami writes:

> It was not naive idealism, it should be recalled, that gave birth to Bush's diplomacy of freedom. That diplomacy issued out of a reading of the Arab-Muslim political condition and of America's vulnerability to the disorder of Arab politics. The ruling regimes in the region had displaced their troubles onto America; their stability had come at America's expense, as the scapegoating and the anti-Americanism had poisoned Arab political life.

Despite Bush's modest framing of the democracy project in Iraq, others have been saying from the very first that the United States has overreached. In promoting democracy universally, the United States has attempted something far beyond its powers. Others say the project is outside the United States' own national interest. As George Washington put it in his Farewell Address (at a time just before the war against the Barbary Pirates), the United States should avoid foreign entanglements:

> It is our true policy to steer clear of permanent alliances with any portion of the foreign world; so far, I mean, as we are now at liberty to do it. . . . Taking care always to keep ourselves by suitable establishments on a respectable defensive posture, we may safely trust to temporary alliances for extraordinary emergencies.
>
> Yet even in Washington's time, American vessels were obliged to go to war to protect distant shipping lanes. It may have been prophetic that America's first foreign war was against Muslim renegades.

4. IS THE NEW STRATEGY TOO LATE?

AFTER THE HIGH POINTS in 2004–2005—the massive "purple finger" elections and the low point of al Qaeda's campaign of terror and disruption—the foes of democracy made a ruthless calculation to escalate their attacks. They bombed several of the most revered Shia mosques, assassinated the most effective local Shia leaders, and turned loose horrific violence in universities, markets, and official buildings around the country, but especially in Baghdad and in Anbar Province to its west. Thousands of civilians were maimed or killed, with many dead bodies left out in the streets as vivid demonstrations of their capacity to inflict pain.

The aim of this campaign was to incite sectarian reprisals and, in turn, a country-wide civil war. It succeeded, inasmuch as Shia death squads very soon began to do to Sunnis what Sunnis were doing to them (most of the foreign terrorists, like Saddam's political musclemen, are Sunnis). During 2006, the underlying tissue of Iraq society began to disintegrate, even though considerable progress was still being made in various sectors. Without physical security for simple daily living, many Iraqis began to feel the cold fear that Saddam Hussein had years ago incited in them.

The Americans had always known that no one but the Iraqis could make democracy work in Iraq. Americans could give them an opportunity, but it could not force Iraqis to fight for democracy and to make democracy work for the common good of all. That is why the downward slide during 2006 caused many Americans to lose heart in the effort being made in Iraq. A weaker administration than Bush's—one merely following polls—might have seized the opportunity to "cut its losses" and head for the exits. This course is what al Qaeda and its allies passionately desired the Americans to take.

President Bush, however, had his sights set on making democracy work in at least one volatile nation in the incendiary Middle East, knowing that the example of one would irrepressibly spread to others. The early defection of Qaddafi, civil unrest in Iran (especially among the young), and the "cedar revolution" in Lebanon made his course seem plausible. He was not yet ready to give up his grand design. In the face of opposition and ridicule from opponents and the press, the President had to remain resolute in his determination to prevail. At times alone, he pressed ahead. Friends write to me that he has been "supercilious, arrogant, unwilling to listen to others, obdurate, misled and stupid." Another description of the same facts is that the President has been uncommonly brave and maintained uncommon inner equanimity. Instead of surrendering, he decided to match the surge of the jihadist haters of democracy with a well-designed surge of his own.

He ordered another five brigades of crack combat troops to Baghdad—with some elements slated for Anbar Province. These were the two most neuralgic points of civilian insecurity and fear. Meanwhile, Iraqi Prime Minister Maliki promised twice that many brigades of the Iraqi Army, each of them at more than 90 percent of full strength—and he delivered. Almost immediately the difference began to be visible.

According to the new coalition commander, General Petraeus, the Army's best expert on counter-insurgency warfare, three early goals had to be met: The Mahdi Army of Sayyid Al Sadr in Sadr City had to be appropriately disarmed. Second, almost eighty command centers had to be established in eighty different Baghdad neighborhoods, so that Iraqi and U.S. forces could secure these neighborhoods by living there, and offer medical services and other basic assistance to their people. Third, the back of the foreign occupation of Anbar Province by al Qaeda had to be snapped. Only in that way could twenty-five tribal sheiks of the area be persuaded to side with the new Iraq democracy, and against the murderous invaders.

By late 2007, General Petraeus was able to report to the Congress that substantial progress had already been made in achieving these goals. Violence was down across Iraq and Iraqi citizens were beginning to cooperate actively with allied troops in the campaign against insurgents. The new strategy was plainly working. The main question was whether or not it came too late to maintain the commitment of the United States to persevere in Iraq. That remains an open question now—and perhaps it will not be settled in any conclusive manner until the 2008 presidential election when the Republican and Democratic candidates will take sharply discordant positions on the Iraq issue

A NUMBER OF MY FRIENDS OPPOSE, and have from the beginning opposed, the "fantasy" of promoting democracy in Iraq. The most bitter of them assert that President Bush is living in a world of delusions and (even worse) lies. They sometimes become passionate in insisting that he "lied" about weapons of mass destruction, and since these WMD were the number one reason given for the war, the whole adventure is based upon this lie. For myself, I remember well President Bush's formal address at the annual banquet of the American Enterprise Institute early in February 2003, just six weeks before the war was launched. It is true that he said about WMD what President Clinton also had said, as well as Senator Clinton, former Vice President Gore, and a virtually unbroken chain of others in a position to know, not only in the U.S. but in Italy, Germany, and France.

But personally, I was convinced about the existence of WMD in Iraq by the January testimony of Hans Blix, the UN inspector of the Iraqi arms programs, to the effect that he knew for certain that 8,500 liters of anthrax known to be in the earlier possession of the Iraqi government now were "unaccounted for." He added in a memorable phrase: "Mustard gas is not like marmalade," it was not simply misplaced, some one has to know where it is, or what had happened to it. The line about marmalade convinced me, and stuck in my memory. I calculated that 8,500 liters of anthrax could be loaded into not much more than two large trailer trucks. Two trucks would not be so hard to hide. In addition, by the terms of the ceasefire agreement of 1991 (which was still the controlling legal authority), the responsibility to account for that missing anthrax lay with the government of Iraq. It was not the responsibility of the nations of the United Nations to go look for it.

If there were no weapons of mass destruction in Iraq, it was the responsibility of the government of Iraq to do what at least a dozen other nations under a similar obligation had done, viz., to prove what had happened to them. Iraq had used WMD before 1991, and an inventory of all it possessed at that time had been in large measure completed not long afterwards. In 2003 the question was: What has happened to them?

Nonetheless, the main stress of the President's long policy address to the AEI that February was not on WMD, but on the need to turn the young people of the Middle East in a new direction, away from repression and submission under draconian dictatorships, in favor of new vital civil societies under democratic regimes committed to human rights and region-wide prosperity. His aim was to replace a politics of bombs, assassinations, and secret police with a politics of public argument, civil persuasion, and economic opportunity. I heard the President elaborate on these ideas about the crucial role of democracy in a new Middle East in addresses to the National Endowment for Democracy, too. It was the salience of the new orientation of the region toward democracy and economic opportunity (not the important but secondary concern with weapons of mass destruction) that distinguished the President's approach.

FOR THESE REASONS, those who blindly shout that the President "lied" are themselves, by knowledge I heard with my own ears, playing fast and loose with the facts. They have blinded themselves, perhaps through their hatred of President Bush. The truth is not on their side.

It may be that the American and Coalition surge of 2007—the surge which ought to have been launched early in 2006, or even earlier—will be too little, too late. There will certainly be a ferocious counter-attack by the enemy. It will be anticipated, and hopefully confronted and decisively defeated, so that we can press forward to accomplish the three main goals that General Petraeus has set forth. What we must not lose sight of is the strategic vision: to launch a free and stable new democracy in the Arab Middle East, as a harbinger of a new flowering of democracy in the least democratic part of the world. Even now Arab scholars publish widely on the "democracy deficit" and "freedom deficit" of the Arab Middle East. Not only for the sake of all the inhabitants of that region, but also for the safety of the rest of us, replacing in the hearts of the Arab young the jihadist passion for destruction, with a new passion for human dignity and prosperity, is the single glimmering hope of the entire region.

Democracy has many faults and many limits, and its success requires the fulfillment of many preconditions. Yet not to get started on the long march toward democracy in the Arab Middle East is to abandon to despair and misery a very large part of the world. It is also to leave untouched a sanguinary vortex of destructive passions, at the central crossroads of the three great land masses on this planet: Asia, Africa, and Europe.

5. THE GREATEST THREAT TO LIBERTY ON EARTH

Islamic terrorism is a new form of political totalitarianism. Although it masks itself in the trappings of a selectively primitive form of Islam, this movement is, once its self-deceiving mask is torn away, primarily political. It is political, military, and totalitarian, as is evident in its express ambitions, its energizing motivations, its ends, its methods. It has no respect for Muslim mosques, or prayer services, or imams, or worshipers; it will destroy them indiscriminately if that is in its temporary military interest. This political movement is fed by fierce resentment of what its members perceive to have been five centuries of subservience to morally inferior Western societies, whose sole temporary advantage is superior technology and productive capacity. Further, according to the testimony of one who became a youthful terrorist before abandoning that path, this political-military movement feeds upon the frustrations of its young males, taught that it is wrong even to masturbate, while daily tantalized by visions of seventy lusty virgins beckoning them into martyrdom. (Furthermore, the practice of polygamy assures that there will never be enough Muslim women to go around.)

Negatively, the jihadist ambition is to reduce to impotence the civilization of freedom. Positively, its ambition is to construct a new Caliphate from Spain to the Sea of Arabia, and from thence eastward to the populous Muslim lands of Asia. As compared with a century ago, the Muslim lands have enormous new wealth from oil reserves, and may soon gain political influence from the development of nuclear weapons. More daringly, therefore, its terrorist visionaries now imagine reducing Europe, Britain, and North America to submission to Allah, either through forced conversion, or through the imposition of *dhimmitude*. *Dhimmitude* is a system of vassalage and systematic humiliation, by which the subservient (unworthy of becoming Muslims) make annual payment of special taxes, to subsidize their own "protection" by the Caliphate.

The most daring jihadists claim that they will reduce much of Europe to vassalage by the year 2030, through the threefold pressure of continued immigration, demographic fertility, and the region-wide radicalization of young males. They see growing signs that internal self-deception and moral decadence are slowly reducing the West to muddle-headedness and impotence. Robert Leiken, writing in *Foreign Affairs*, seems to have reached the same conclusion:

> As a consequence of demography, history, ideology, and policy, western Europe now plays host to often disconsolate Muslim offspring, who are its citizens in name but not culturally or socially. In a fit of absent-mindedness, Western Europe acquired not a colonial empire but something of an internal colony, whose numbers are roughly equivalent to the population of Syria.

Meanwhile, a few powerful Middle Eastern states are secretly stimulating, supporting, and prompting terrorist cells (and even small armies) in a drip-drip of violent attacks upon the civilization of freedom. Central among these sponsors of terrorism is oil-rich

Iran, newly wealthy heir of the ancient Persian Empire. With the assistance of Syria, Iran is fomenting discord, violence, anarchy, and terror in every nation on its borders. Its current principal targets are the fragile democracies in Lebanon and Palestine. But its most vital target is Iraq. Iran cannot allow its hereditary enemy to succeed with a new democratic experiment; that would quickly destabilize its own still fragile and unpopular Islamist dictatorship. Furthermore, successful democracy in Iraq would suck the vitality out of Iran's campaign of terror in the region. The success of the democracy experiment in Iraq would threaten the foundational pillars of the Iranian regime.

Iran may be the financial capital and militant, terrorist center of the international movement of Muslim supremacy. Decade by decade, more and more countries place themselves under Sharia law, as Iran has, as the Taliban had imposed upon Afghanistan, as the Sudan has, as half of Nigeria already has (while the other half quakes). Politicized, militarized versions of Islam keep spreading internationally—in Britain, in the Netherlands, in Indonesia, in Denmark and Sweden, in France, in Germany, in Argentina, and to some unknown extent in hidden, small communities elsewhere. Demography is destiny; successful and law-abiding democracies provide warm shelter, and immigration gives international propulsion to the steady infiltration of democratic societies. Worldwide Muslim populations increase and multiply. So do communities of Muslims within ever more nations. The Minarets that Edward Gibbon once imagined rising over Oxford had the triumphant Muslim invasion of France not been halted by Charles the Hammer (Charles Martel) at Tours in 732 A.D. are now arising there peacefully, under the summer sun and a comfortable breeze.

THIRTEEN CENTURIES after Charles Martel's surprising victory, the strong horse of Islamic militancy can foresee Sharia Law pushing aside the weak horse of the Common Law, not only in motor vehicle offices, and immigration offices, and multi-cultural offices, and university offices, but in more and more other departments of the common life. By 2032, like a frog who never felt the warm water slowly coming to a boil, important states of Europe may well be living under the Minarets as, in his acute imagination, Edward Gibbon long ago foresaw.

There are many in the West today who do not see Islamofascism as a threat. They deny that the West is now engaged in the most deadly form of warfare that it has ever faced, against the most stealthy and relentless foe. Like frogs in the pot, they deny that they are in peril. They regard the war in Iraq as Al Gore put it in December 2006, "the worst strategic mistake in the history of the United States." They do not see the strategic wisdom in halting the simmering resentment among the young in worldwide Islamic communities by turning youthful idealism toward creative social visions, building new Islamic cultures based upon the rule of law, the equality of all, and upon dynamic, inventive, free economies to support democratic institutions.

Islamic cultures are today awash with oil wealth which they use to support armies and arms programs, and, even, nuclear weapons. Their weakness lies in their failure to inspire economic enterprise and democratic love for the rule of law. They do nothing for the dignity of individuals, nothing to protect their individual rights. That is why so many Muslim nations seethe with internal discontent which has few constructive channels for expression. These societies thus invite domination by new forms of tyranny. To all these deformations, the dream of democracy and creative enterprise is a bewitching counterpoise.

The success or failure of the democratic experiment in Iraq is, therefore, of world-historical importance. Therein will be decided which one is the strong horse, by nature attracting people's allegiance, and which is the weak horse, passively kneeling down as it awaits the drawn knives.

June 2007

The Case for Freedom

Natan Sharansky and Rod Dermer

Democracy has not failed in the Middle East, argue Natan Sharansky and Rod Dermer, but rather it has not been promoted and defended with the seriousness and patience that the enterprise requires. President Bush was correct to say that the promotion of democracy around the world is vital to America's security—and to the security of peace-loving nations around the globe. The violence and terror that are common in the region arise from the absence of democratic rule. Democratic governments succeed by promoting freedom and prosperity among their people, while tyrannies succeed by controlling their people. This lack of opportunity, they argue, provokes resentment and extremism in the region. Democracy and freedom are the answer to this challenge—but success in this enterprise will require a sustained commitment on the part of the United States because powerful interests in the region will fight to maintain the status quo.

IN HIS FIRST INAUGURAL ADDRESS, George W. Bush offered no sign of the sweeping democracy rhetoric that has marked his presidency, limiting himself only to this detached observation: "Through much of the last century, America's faith in freedom and democracy was a rock in a raging sea. Now it is a seed upon the wind, taking root in many nations." One could hardly think of a more passive image for spreading freedom around the globe.

The new president did warn "the enemies of liberty" that America was committed to "shaping a balance of power that favors freedom," but couched in language that could have been penned in any European foreign office, Bush's words ruffled no feathers. In his Second Inaugural, however, President Bush championed democracy as few leaders ever have, pledging that America would "seek and support the growth of democratic movements and institutions in every nation and culture, with the ultimate goal of ending tyranny in our world." Though calling this ambitious endeavor "the concentrated work of generations," he boldly declared that his administration would "encourage reform in other governments by making clear that success in our relations will require the decent treatment of their own people." If non-democratic regimes were put on notice, the president's message to those they persecuted was even clearer:

> All who live in tyranny and hopelessness can know: the United States government will not ignore your oppression, or excuse your oppressors. When you stand for your liberty, we will stand with you. Democratic reformers facing repression, prison, or exile can know: America sees you for who you are: the future leaders of your free country.

The man who had once called for a "humble" foreign policy had now committed America to "ending tyranny in our world." What happened?

The obvious answer is 9/11. But did the horrific carnage of that day necessitate such a dramatic change in American policy? Couldn't the U.S. have prosecuted the war on terror differently? Couldn't it have ousted the Taliban, or even Saddam Hussein, without replacing them with democratic regimes?

A closer inspection of Bush's speech reveals the post-9/11 logic behind the democracy policy:

We have seen our vulnerability—and *we have seen its deepest source* [emphasis added]. For as long as whole regions of the world simmer in resentment and tyranny—prone to ideologies that feed hatred and excuse murder—violence will gather, and multiply in destructive power, and cross the most defended borders and raise a mortal threat. There is only one force of history that can break the reign of hatred and resentment, and expose the pretensions of tyrants, and reward the hopes of the decent and tolerant, and that is the force of human freedom. We are led by events and common sense to one conclusion: The survival of liberty in our land increasingly depends on the success of liberty in other lands. The best hope for peace in our world is the expansion of freedom in all the world.

The president based his democracy initiative on the conviction that what had led to 9/11, and what continued to pose a "mortal threat" to the United States, was a byproduct of non-democratic rule. This threat, the logic went, could only be neutralized by promoting the very force—freedom—whose absence had generated the pathologies in the first place.

Unlike most of his Democratic and Republican predecessors who thought promoting democracy abroad was consonant with American *values* but not necessarily with American *interests*, President Bush called the advance of freedom "an urgent requirement of our nation's security." To Bush, "America's vital interests and our deepest beliefs are now one."

But is President Bush correct? Is American security truly endangered by the absence of freedom in the Middle East?

RESTATING THE CASE FOR DEMOCRACY

THE MECHANICS OF TYRANNY in "fear" societies, where meaningful dissent is not permitted, translates into terror both inside and outside those societies. Contrary to popular belief, the key difference between free and fear societies is not the motives of their leaders nor the virtues of their populations: Evil transcends borders, and nearly all those in power are determined to wield it as long as possible.

The difference lies instead in the systems in which these leaders operate: In free societies, leaders depend on the people; in fear societies, people depend on their leaders. So while the power of democratic leaders is largely a function of the degree of *support* they enjoy among their citizens, the power of non-democratic leaders is a function of the degree of *control* they exert over their subjects.

In free societies, leaders maintain support over time by delivering peace and prosperity. While voters will support the deprivations of war if it is absolutely necessary, democratic leaders will not remain in office for long, or will exhaust their political capital very quickly, if they support wars the public does not regard as vital to the national interest.

In fear societies, leaders stay in power by retaining control over their populations. Exerting this control becomes increasingly difficult as popular discontent invariably grows over time. More and more subjects turn from "true believers," who genuinely support the ideology of the regime, into "doublethinkers," who parrot that ideology out of fear but no longer believe it.

To keep control over the growing ranks of doublethinkers, and to ensure they do not cross the line into open dissent, the regime must resort to ever stronger means of repression. They kill and imprison dissidents, empower a secret police, and indoctrinate the masses. Inevitably, these regimes also try to consolidate their control by uniting their subjects against a real or imagined enemy. Though Stalin, Hitler, and Saddam ruled very different countries representing vastly diverse cultures, they all understood that manufacturing enemies was critical to maintaining their grip on power—an understanding not lost on the likes of Kim Jong-il, Bashar Assad, and Fidel Castro.

Though their rulers' lengthy tenure and the repression they are willing to countenance make fear societies appear "stable," they are powder kegs of popular resentment. Unwilling to construct the type of society that would redress grievances peacefully, these regimes specialize in diverting popular discontent by fomenting a fanatical hatred of others and by mobilizing people for war. That is why Andrei Sakharov used to say that regimes that do not respect the rights of their own people will never respect the rights of their neighbors, and why such regimes threaten both their own subjects and the world.

The threat once posed by tyranny in one particular region of the world was far less serious than it is today. The fires of hatred kindled in fear societies once moved no faster than the speed of a horse. Today, they move as fast as a commercial jet or supersonic missile. Worse, weapons of mass death magnify the dangers exponentially since today's petty tyrant or terrorist can cause destruction on a scale that yesterday's great power could scarcely imagine.

WHAT ABOUT ISLAM?

STILL, SOME COGNIZANT OF THE THREATS from the region may nonetheless think that focusing on democracy misses the point. Many see Islamic fanaticism as the "deepest source" of the problem. The real threat, they argue, comes not from the authoritarian, secular rule of the Mubaraks, Arafats, and Assads but from the religious fanaticism of al Qaeda, Hamas, and Iran.

Admittedly, everywhere one looks, from Bali to Baghdad, from Jerusalem to Madrid, from London to New York, terrorism is perpetrated in the name of Islam. A virulent strain of Islam that has gained much wider currency in the Middle East in the past generation openly seeks to restore Islam's lost dominance, re-establish the Caliphate, and ultimately subdue the world under Sharia law.

But the virulence of the Islamist threat both inside and outside the Middle East is linked to the region's freedom-deficit. By failing to provide their people with freedom and opportunity, by controlling subjects rather than serving citizens, the autocrats that litter the region have encouraged people to turn elsewhere for solutions. In building schools, running health clinics, and providing food for the poor, Islamist groups have stepped into the vacuum and increased their support dramatically. This formula has proven effective for Shiite and Sunni fundamentalist groups alike.

Yet the provision of these services comes with a heavy price tag. Islamists use them as conduits for indoctrinating recipients into a twisted view of the world that demonizes Jews, Christians, Israel, America, and the West—propaganda that echoes the poison broadcast daily through the "secular" controlled media. Though the region's secular autocrats and religious fanatics differ on the appropriate solution to their problems, they largely agree on who is to blame.

If the Middle East were free, fewer would turn to the mosque for solutions to the region's lack of development because there would be development. People would not have to go to Islamists to provide basic services because governments accountable to the people would provide those services. Most important, the capacity of mosques and madrasses to indoctrinate the masses would be seriously diminished.

But doesn't the threat from Islamic fanaticism extend beyond the Middle East? Would bringing democracy to the Middle East end the Islamist threat in France, Holland, or Britain?

To be sure, the alienation felt by many Muslim immigrants in the West, which has made them easy prey for Islamist preachers, appears to have little to do with the state of democracy in the Middle East. But this is not simply a homegrown phenomenon.

Islamists, unlike Americans, are not shy about exporting their values. For decades, Saudi Arabia has spread Wahhabism, its radical state-religion, through a network of mosques it finances in Europe, Asia, and even America. Bernard Lewis, perhaps the foremost authority on Islam, explains the growth of Wahabbism:

> Imagine that the Ku Klux Klan gets total control of Texas, and
> that the Ku Klux Klan has at its disposal all the oil rigs in Texas.

And they use this money to set up a well-endowed network of colleges and schools throughout Christendom, peddling their peculiar brand of Christianity. You would then have an approximate equivalent to what has happened in the modern Muslim world.

Not only is much of the growth of Islamism in the West fueled by forces that originate in the Middle East, the strength of those forces is directly related to the freedom deficit in the region. In the case of Saudi Arabia, a regime without popular support has bought its legitimacy by supporting Wahhabism inside the Kingdom and by financing its export.

Like fascism, Islamism is best cultivated in tyranny. Should the spark of freedom ignite in the Middle East, the strength of Islamist forces there would be sharply reduced, as would their influence elsewhere. Just as the collapse of the Soviet Union largely eliminated the dangers of Communist movements around the world, so too when the Islamist threat is eliminated in the region, it will no longer pose a threat to the world.

IS A DEMOCRATIC MIDDLE EAST POSSIBLE?

ARE SOME PEOPLES OR CULTURES simply incompatible with democratic life? To most observers, what is happening in Iraq, Afghanistan, Lebanon, the Palestinian-controlled areas, and elsewhere in the Middle East inspires little confidence that free societies in the region have a future.

But just as the best experts were wrong when they insisted that democracy would never take root in Germany, Japan, Spain, Latin America, and the former Soviet Union, those who believe it cannot take root in the Middle East will be proven wrong as well. True, every case of democracy's successful emergence is unique. Some point to a pervasive sense of defeat inside Japan, a strong middle class in Germany, an educated population in Eastern Europe, or a number of other factors as essential predicates to democracy which are absent in the Middle East today. Undoubtedly, until Arabs build a successful democratic polity, skepticism will remain.

Yet look at what has happened since 9/11. From the millions of Iraqis who voted despite death threats to the hundreds of thousands of Lebanese who initiated the Cedar Revolution to the 4,000 Egyptian judges who bravely challenged authoritarian rule, the last few years have born witness to an unprecedented awakening of freedom in the Arab world. Though the road to democracy has certainly been rocky, what has happened over the last five years does not mean that Arabs are incapable of building a free society any more than the Reign of Terror or two centuries of slavery meant that the French or Americans were incapable of building a free society.

To lose heart about the possibility of a democratic Middle East would be very short-sighted. These problems in the region are not evidence that Arabs are incapable of building free societies but rather evidence that such societies would pose a mortal threat to the forces of tyranny and terror in the region.

We should be under no illusions. Not a single non-democratic regime wants America to succeed in advancing democracy because these regimes recognize that their own repressive rule would thereby be endangered. Iran and Syria are helping to fuel the carnage in Iraq because they correctly understand that America's victory there would be their defeat. To assume they will help America is to assume they would willingly sign their own death warrant. Similarly, the forces of terror in the region, from al Qaeda to Hezbollah to Hamas, understand that the swamps in which they breed will begin to drain if Afghans, Iraqis, Lebanese, Palestinians, or anyone else can build a free society, and they will do whatever it takes to prevent that from happening.

Mr. Bush deserves much credit for recognizing how important spreading democracy in the Middle East is to the *security* of his country and the world, and any criticism we have about the failure to consistently and forcefully implement the democracy agenda is tempered by our appreciation for his having embraced such an agenda in the first place. But in briefly surveying the places in the region where democracy has ostensibly been put to the test, what one sees is not that democracy has failed but rather that it has been rarely pursued in practice.

PALESTINIAN-CONTROLLED TERRITORIES

IRONICALLY, THE IMPORTANCE of building free societies has been most thoroughly ignored on Israel's own democratic doorstep. The Oslo peace process drew no link between freedom and peace. On the contrary, it was based on the idea that a strong dictator was critical to peace. As former Prime Minister Yitzhak Rabin put it, Arafat would confront Hamas without the constraints of "a Supreme Court, human rights organizations and all kinds of bleeding heart liberals."

After the failure of the Camp David talks in the summer of 2000 and the outbreak of the Palestinian terror war that followed, President Bush boldly decided to break with the logic of Oslo. In June 2002, he made clear to the Palestinian leadership "that success in our relations will require the decent treatment of their own people."

> I call on the Palestinians to build a practicing democracy,
> based on tolerance and liberty. *If* the Palestinian people actively
> pursue these goals, America and the world will actively support
> their efforts. . . . *If* Palestinians embrace democracy, confront
> corruption and firmly reject terror, they can count on American
> support for the creation of a provisional state of Palestine.
> [Emphasis added.]

But as Bush conditioned American support for Palestinian statehood on the Palestinians' willingness to build a free society, his administration helped formulate a Road Map that precluded any such possibility. By calling for elections "as soon as possible" and paying mere lip service to democratic reforms, the Road Map ensured that actual reform would never happen.

This should have been obvious to anyone following what was happening in the Palestinian Authority for the last decade. The dangers of holding an election *before* reforms were implemented in a corrupt society poisoned by incitement were plain to see. Yet barely a day goes by when someone does not point out that the election of Hamas *proves* that the democracy agenda was a catastrophic mistake. But what brought Hamas to power was not democracy but the foolish decision to hold quick elections in a fear society in the wake of a misguided withdrawal. In fact, *four* years before those elections, we warned against the Road Map's provision for quick elections: "Rather than call for elections at the beginning of the process of reform," we wrote, "elections must *only* come after that process is well underway." And in our book, published more than a year before Hamas came to power, we further explained:

> Only when the basic institutions that protect a free society
> are in place—such as a free press, the rule of law, independent
> courts, political parties—can free elections be held. After
> defeating Hitler, the United States and allied occupation forces
> wisely postponed federal elections in Germany for four years.
> Had elections been held in 1945 or 1946, the results probably
> would have undermined efforts to build German democracy,
> something those who hope to build democratic societies in
> Afghanistan and Iraq would be wise to keep in mind. . . .

In short, the election of Hamas was the logical consequence of a decade-old failure to help Palestinians build a free society. Rather than the free world, including Israel, using all of our considerable leverage over a Palestinian regime entirely dependent on our support in order to strengthen Palestinian civil society and improve Palestinian lives, we turned a blind eye as Palestinian civil society was hollowed out, the Palestinian economy was monopolized by thugs, and a generation of Palestinian children were indoctrinated into a culture that glorified martyrdom and death. If instead of simply holding an election, a multi-year effort had been made to institute real democratic reforms, detoxify a poisoned population, and dismantle refugee camps, a genuine peace process could have begun.

If the Bush administration is serious about the Palestinians building "a practicing democracy, based on tolerance and liberty," it should be reaching out to the many Palestinian individuals and groups that want to be partners in building such a society. They can begin to do that by denying legitimacy to leaders who refuse to end incitement, earmarking funds to help Palestinian businessmen establish an independent economic existence, and mobilizing international support for a program to provide Palestinians living in refugee camps with decent housing.

Instead, the administration appears headed back down the path of Oslo by facilitating the latest diplomatic initiative, the so-called Saudi peace plan. Five years after boldly breaking with an Oslo logic that ignored democracy, is the Bush administration now placing its faith in the most anti-democratic regime in the region to implement Bush's vision of two democratic states living side by side?

If the free world, led by the United States, begins to insist that success in its relations with the Palestinians "requires the decent treatment of their own people," and if democratic Palestinian reformers, of which there are many, believe that America regards them as "the future leaders of [their] free country," a real peace process can finally begin. If not, all efforts to make peace, sincere as they may be, will remain nothing more than an illusion.

IRAN

THE REGIME IN TEHRAN is one of the most dangerous in the world. President Mahmoud Ahmadinejad, an apocalyptic fanatic who believes it is his duty to hasten the arrival of the Shiite Messiah, brazenly denies the Holocaust and pledges to "wipe Israel off the map." According to his twisted worldview, Israel, "the little Satan," is merely an appetizer. For Ahmadinejad and the Iranian mullahs, who ask their adherents to "imagine a world without America," the United States is the "Great Satan."

While the regime's rhetoric is frightening, its actions are every bit as alarming. It provides hundreds of millions of dollars, weapons, and training to Hezbollah, which before 9/11 had the distinction of killing more Americans than any other terror organization. After spending many years sponsoring Islamic Jihad, one of the deadliest Palestinian terror groups, and after trying to send arms to Arafat on the infamous Karine A, Iran has now become a major backer of Hamas.

Iran has also been working to undermine coalition efforts in Iraq. The IED roadside explosives responsible for the majority of American casualties in Iraq are mostly imported from Iran, and the regime sponsors Shiite death squads and radical anti-American clerics like Muqhta Al Sadr.

Worst of all, Iran is feverishly pursuing nuclear weapons. With missiles that can already reach deep into Europe and with the potential to pass nuclear weapons on to proxies like Hezbollah and others, a nuclear Iran would be a danger to the entire free world.

Yet there are few places in the world more ripe for democratic change than Iran. Nearly three decades after the Islamic Revolution, the Iranian people are nearly all doublethinkers. Increasingly, trade unions, student organizations, and women's groups are openly expressing their opposition to the regime. Indeed, what is happening in Iran today can be analogized to the Solidarity Movement in Poland.

The difference is this: When the Solidarity Movement emerged, its leaders became heroes in the West, won a Nobel Prize, and the Pope championed their cause. As a result, the Soviets came under intense international pressure.

In contrast, the free world has largely ignored the Iranian democratic movement. Though President Bush has used his pulpit to speak directly to Iranian democrats and has called for the release of prominent Iranian dissidents, his administration has not provided any meaningful financial support to them. When former Pennsylvania Sen. Rick Santorum tried to pass legislation last year earmarking $100 million for the Iranian democratic opposition, the State Department actively campaigned to defeat it.

Remarkably, many who seek to "engage" Iran today have used the Cold War to buttress their position. "If we spoke to the Soviets," their argument goes, "we should speak to the Iranians." But what these policymakers ignore is that the Soviets saw detente as an opportunity to clamp down on dissent at home and expand their influence abroad. It was only when leaders like "Scoop" Jackson and Ronald Reagan reversed these efforts that the entire dynamic of the Cold War changed.

Many today believe that the collapse of the Soviet Union was inevitable because of its weak economy. It is interesting that none of the so-called experts predicted the inevitable before it happened. Sure, the Soviet economy was weak, but non-democratic regimes have been able to rule weak economies without collapsing for decades (North Korea and Cuba are but two examples). The reason the USSR collapsed is that President Reagan and others exploited that weakness by increasing pressure on the regime. They did so not only by rebuilding their defenses but also by linking the relationship with the Soviet Union to the question of human rights. They recognized that the greatest weapon in the West's arsenal was the desire for freedom burning inside those behind the Iron Curtain. So too, America's most powerful weapon today against Tehran is the Iranian people.

The free world must make clear to Ahmadinejad that his regime will get no legitimacy and no economic support if it continues its current policies. In addition to confronting the Iranian terror network, the free world should also subject the regime to international censure (such as trying Ahmadinejad for incitement to genocide), and economic pressures (such as divesting from companies that do business in Iran). And just as Radio Free Europe and Voice of America once amplified the calls for freedom that were being raised inside the Soviet Union, the same should be done to amplify the calls for freedom inside Iran. As former Iranian student leader and political prisoner Amir-Abbas Fakhravar explained, "Iranians themselves need to know that the outside world is interested in them and wants to help them. . . . Information has to be disbursed so that the people of Tehran will go out in the streets like the people of Lebanon and Ukraine."

LEBANON

LEBANON REPRESENTS both America's greatest success and greatest failure: success, because nowhere was the United States able to effect such dramatic change with so little effort; failure, because rather than help secure Lebanon's democratic future, America backed away.

Only three weeks after Bush's Second Inaugural address, Prime Minister Rafik Hariri was assassinated. In the Cedar Revolution that followed, hundreds of thousands of Lebanese demonstrated against Assad's regime demanding that it end its three-decade occupation of Lebanon. Within a month, the Syrian military was forced to leave.

When asked how important Bush's support of democracy was to their efforts, one leading organizer of the rally described it as "absolutely critical." Like many protesters, he assumed that America would not allow the Syrians to do what the Chinese had done fifteen years earlier to pro-democracy protesters in Tiananmen Square. They believed that this time, America would indeed "stand with those who stood for liberty."

But America did not capitalize on the considerable momentum of the Syrian withdrawal to strengthen democratic forces inside Lebanon and to insist that Hezbollah disarm as called for in UN resolution 1559. Instead, Hezbollah was allowed to participate in elections, and the U.S. supported its inclusion in a national unity government. Thus Hezbollah, financed and supported by Iran and Syria, remained in control of southern Lebanon.

The failure to confront Hezbollah would prove costly. On July 12, 2006, Hezbollah crossed an internationally recognized border, kidnapped two Israeli soldiers, killed several others, and fired rockets on Israeli cities. Israel responded by targeting Hezbollah missile batteries, strongholds, and fighters. In the resulting war, 4,000 missiles were fired at Israel, and 150 Israelis were killed. On the Lebanese side, over 600 Hezbollah terrorists were killed, as were many innocent Lebanese who were being used as human shields by terrorists embedded in civilian areas.

Today, the United States appears to understand that Hezbollah must not be appeased and is therefore providing economic and military support to democratic forces within Lebanon. This support is sorely needed since Hezbollah continues to violate last summer's cease-fire by replenishing its weapons stocks and is actively trying to oust Lebanon's democratically minded government.

The lesson of Lebanon, then, is not that democracy cannot be built in the Middle East, but rather that it will not be built without a fight. While America stayed largely on the sidelines, Iran and Syria spent hundreds of millions of dollars, supplied weapons, and sent in trained fighters in order to snuff out democracy in Lebanon. With only a fraction of the resources dedicated elsewhere in the region, America could have helped build a truly free Lebanon, marginalized Hezbollah, and reduced the influence of Iran. Luckily for all of us, there is still time to do so.

Far from providing evidence of the failure of democracy in the Middle East, the three regions above show that a sustained policy of promoting democracy has either been totally rejected (Palestinian areas), largely ignored (Iran), or haphazardly pursued (Lebanon). Not surprisingly, when America has rejected or ignored democracy, the results have been disastrous, and when it appears serious about advancing democratic reform, we have glimpsed the possibility of a genuinely transformed Middle East.

IRAQ

RIGHT OR WRONG, the central theater for testing a vision of a democratic Middle East is Iraq. There have been moments when that vision seemed closer to fruition, such as when millions of Iraqis proudly displayed their purple fingers after voting in the Arab world's first democratic elections. But time after time, violence dashed hopes of a better future. Today, after four years, 3,000 American casualties, tens of thousands of Iraqi dead, hundreds of billions of dollars expended, and sectarian violence that shows no signs of abating, many believe that the prospects for a democratic Iraq have never been dimmer.

Making America's task exponentially more difficult are those inside and outside Iraq who are determined to see democracy fail, from the thousands of Baathist insurgents hoping to restore their former dominance to neighboring regimes trying to foment instability and chaos to an international terror movement that has declared war on what Musab al-Zarqawi called "this evil principle of democracy."

If a democratic Iraq is to overcome these obstacles, it will be because of people like Mithal-Al-Alusi, a Sunni Muslim who is a member of Iraq's new parliament. In 2005, two of Alusi's sons were gunned down in what was one of many attempts on his life. A few hours after the attack, Alusi had this to say on Radio Free Europe:

> Again, henchmen of the Ba'ath [Party] and dirty terrorist gangs,
> Al-Qaeda and others, are going out convinced that they can
> determine life and death as they desire.... We will not, [I swear]
> by God, hand over Iraq to murderers and terrorists.... We want
> to build Iraq; there has been enough destruction. We want to
> build schools for Iraqis, hospitals for Iraqis, and state institu-

tions. We will not allow Iraq to become a tool in the hands of others.

During the Cold War, many dismissed the voices of dissidents behind the Iron Curtain. Many will similarly dismiss Alusi as a lone voice in a sea of fanaticism. But like all peoples liberated from tyranny, most Iraqis will never want to be slaves again. Democracy in Iraq is possible because so many Iraqis want to be free and because the leader of the free world has not abandoned them to face the enemies of freedom alone.

But while a free Iraq is possible, it is not inevitable. For men like Alusi to succeed, security must be restored, those inside Iraq determined to undermine democracy must be confronted, neighboring regimes sowing chaos must be deterred and al Qaeda terrorists operating in Iraq will have to be brought to justice.

We certainly hope President Bush's new plan will succeed in accomplishing these objectives. But even if those hopes are not fulfilled, American leaders should not make the dangerous mistake of throwing out the democratic baby with the Iraqi bathwater.

Before abandoning democracy in the Middle East, we must recognize that what has made building a free Iraq so difficult is not that Iraqis do not want freedom but rather that the lasting effects of three decades of Saddam's savage rule, centuries of mistrust between Sunni and Shiites, and an entrenched tribalism that often trumps identity with the Iraqi nation-state have made it difficult for sectarian groups to resolve their differences. Just because most Iraqi Sunnis, Shiites, and Kurds want to *live free* does not necessarily mean that they want to *live together*.

Witness Yugoslavia: A country of profound ethnic divisions once held together by a dictator was torn apart by ethnic hatreds. But the question of whether Bosnians, Serbs and Croats could build free societies was a separate question from whether they were willing to live in one country. Even in places where ethnic hatreds have been muted, communities have preferred to live separately, such as in Czechoslovakia. The Czech and Slovak peoples did not want to share a state together, but they still wanted to live apart in freedom.

The borders that are meant to unite Iraqis reflect the marking of British imperialists, not the history or heritage of an "Iraqi nation." The question is whether after nearly a century of colonial rule and decades of dictatorship, Iraqis have built a common identity that can withstand the centrifugal pressures of enmity and grievance.

Shiites, Kurds, and Sunnis may yet come to the conclusion that their interests are better served by living together. Each community has genuine reasons to fear a break-up of Iraq: Shiites fear domination by a theocratic Iran, Sunnis fear being cut off from oil reserves in the south, and Kurds fear a potential Turkish invasion. And all groups have reason to fear that Iraq's break-up will look more like Yugoslavia than Czechoslovakia.

Some have argued for a "friendly strongman" who will keep Iraq united and "stable." But Saddam was once considered a "friendly strongman," and he murdered hundreds of thousands of Iraqis, persecuted millions more, started two wars, and sponsored terror in the region. If this is the price for "stability" and unity, its price is far too high for Iraqis, for their neighbors, and for the world.

Hopefully, men like Mr. Alusi will succeed in building a free and united Iraq. But if the choice is between democracy without Iraq or Iraq without democracy, then Shiites, Sunnis, and Kurds would be better served and the security of the world better protected with the former. If President Bush is right that the "mortal threats" to his country come from "regions that simmer in resentment and tyranny," the question of keeping Iraq together is much less important than the question of whether those who live on its territory are able to live in free societies.

By far the worst of all possible scenarios is for America simply to turn its back on democracy in Iraq and thereby hand the enemies of freedom a great victory. The shock waves of that victory would reverberate for decades to come, emboldening terrorists, strengthening tyrants, undermining America's allies, and, ultimately, endangering America.

THE CHALLENGE AHEAD

IRONICALLY, THE GREATEST CHALLENGE to promoting democracy comes from the land where freedom's torch has always burned brightest and where, sadly, many have now lost faith in the power of freedom to change the world.

President Bush can certainly be criticized for not forging a bipartisan consensus around his democracy agenda, especially given how vital he believes that agenda is to American security. In failing to forge that consensus, Bush has ceded the ground to democracy's skeptics. Whether those skeptics are called "realists" or something else is immaterial for they all worship the same false god of "stability." They counsel backing friendly dictators and calibrating the proper balance of power that can best preserve the status quo.

But make no mistake about it. This approach is not new. It last held sway on September 10, 2001, and was jettisoned only after a horrific attack discredited the status quo in the Middle East. Tragically, judging from the many recommendations of last year's Iraq Study Group that would reward tyrants, court dictators, and abandon democracy, it appears to be the "new" bipartisan consensus.

The current attempt to divide the world into moderates and extremists is further evidence of pre-9/11 thinking. When it comes to the Middle East, this view pits so-called "moderate" regimes like Jordan, Egypt, Saudi Arabia, as well as Palestinian president Abu Mazen, against the extremist regimes in Tehran and Damascus and extremist organizations like al Qaeda, Hezbollah, and Hamas.

But by what possible definition can anyone call the Saudi regime moderate? Because of the rights it affords women? Because of the religious freedom it permits? Because Wahhabism promotes world peace?

The Saudis, as well as the regimes in Egypt and Jordan, do share an interest with America in confronting a growing Iranian menace. But did Stalin's shared interest with the West in confronting Hitler make him a "moderate"?

In the end, the United States may decide to work temporarily with some non-democratic regimes in an effort to confront even greater and more immediate threats to its security. Such was the basis of the WWII alliance with Stalin and with America's support for some dictatorships during the Cold War.

But America must not forget that these regimes are a danger to their own people and to international peace and security. Just as Stalin's cooperation against Hitler did not prevent the Soviet dictator from destroying democracy in Eastern Europe, working with the Saudis to thwart Iranian ambitions will not turn that tyranny into an ally for building democracy in Iraq, Lebanon, the Palestinian-controlled territories, or anywhere else for that matter.

Today, the Saudis may stand with the U.S. in confronting Iran. Tomorrow, terrorists educated in its schools or in the madrasses it finances abroad may attack America. Will the Saudis then cease being "moderates"? Moderation is a function of the degree of freedom a regime affords its citizens. To call countries that have no respect for human rights "moderate" is to abandon the moral clarity that will be essential if we are serious about "ending tyranny in our world."

WE ARE CONVINCED that there is ultimately no alternative to the course President Bush has championed these past few years. Surely, there is no single formula for success that will work in every place at every time. Even those fervently committed to a goal can have strong disagreements over the best way to achieve it. But the idea that America, and by extension the democratic world, can largely ignore the pathologies that tyranny has bred in the Middle East is a dangerous illusion.

September 11 was supposed to change how most people saw the world. It didn't. With more and more policymakers abandoning the idea of promoting democracy, the American people and free people everywhere are fortunate that the Oval Office is occupied by a man who recognizes that the "survival of liberty at home increasingly depends on the success of liberty abroad." We hope that in his remaining time in office, he will succeed in getting his administration to translate his rhetoric more effectively and consistently into policy. We also hope that his successor, Republican or Democrat, will possess similar foresight and courage. For only when liberty is on the march are all those who cherish it more secure.

(May 2007)

Armies for Democracy— Past, Present, and Future

Victor Davis Hanson

Though military conquest is usually associated with dictatorship and, further, democracies are typically suspicious of military power, Victor Davis Hanson reminds us that the great victories of liberal democracy over the past two centuries were only achieved through the application of military power. There exists, as he argues, a proud tradition of "military liberalism" that is greatly responsible for the freedoms we enjoy today. "We sometimes forget," he argues, "that the existential evils of the nineteenth and twentieth centuries—chattel slavery, Nazism, Italian Fascism, Japanese militarism, and Soviet Stalinism—were not only eliminated by force or the threat of force, but exclusively by the might of democratically governed militaries." He cautions that the difficulties of the intervention in Iraq threatens to bring this tradition to an end—which would mean that the United States and its allies will no longer be prepared in the future to use military force to achieve democratic goals. This, he suggests, would be a tragedy, not only for us but for those whom we might otherwise have sought to liberate.

I. DISTRUSTING THE MILITARY

THE COMPLEX AND SOMEWHAT ill-defined relationship between the military establishment and constitutional government is a subject that has made many Americans uncomfortable, especially in the modern era when the United States has assumed a leadership role in world affairs. American Cold War era culture, after all, cautioned us about the intrinsic anti-democratic nature of top-ranking military officers, whether in cinematic portrayals like *Seven Days in May* or *Doctor Strangelove* or the very real inflammatory politicking of retired generals like Douglas MacArthur, Curtis LeMay, or Edwin Walker.

In reaction to these Cold War and Vietnam-era fears, scholars such as Samuel P. Huntington (*The Soldier and the State*) and, more recently, Eliot Cohen (*Supreme Command*) have written insightfully about the proper relationship between civilian and military authorities in a constitutional democracy like ours. These scholars generally agree that the delicate balance was sometimes upset in our past wars when politicians did not have much knowledge about military affairs. Sometimes, out of insecurity, they blustered and bullied officers, or at other times, in recognition of their own ignorance, civilian leaders ceded too much control to the Pentagon.

Under the Clinton administration it was felt that an increasingly alienated military exercised too much autonomy, whether in lecturing civilian authorities that gays simply would not work as fully accepted members of the armed forces or in voicing strong initial opposition to the prospect of humanitarian intervention in the Balkans. Militaries for their part understand that during "peacekeeping" exercises the rules of engagement change, the cameras intrude, and they are asked to assume civilian roles where their target profile increases, while their ability to fight back without restrictions is checked.

During the current Bush presidency, by contrast, the charge was often just the opposite: a compliant Pentagon had been bullied by its civilian overseers into keeping quiet about doubts over the feasibility of neoconservative nation-building. In fact, in 2006 we witnessed a "revolt of the generals" against civilian leadership of the Pentagon. Top brass came forward out of recent retirement to lambaste Secretary of Defense Donald Rumsfeld over the entire civilian conduct of the war in Iraq. They complained that there had been too much micromanagement of the war, too many policy demands placed on a military that was stretched too thin by the requirements of the war, and too much utopian ideology guiding the conduct of the war at the expense of realistic judgments of what in fact was possible.

This insurrection of top retired officers was not quite unprecedented, except in the left's sudden muted silence in response to this rare emergence of like-minded critics of the policy in Iraq. Instead, it was more reminiscent of an earlier "revolt of the admirals" in 1949–50. At that time, in the early years of the Cold War, threatened postwar cutbacks in naval operations led to a similar expression of public outrage by admirals against their civilian overseers. The controversy brought down Secretary of Defense Louis Johnson and led to firings and resignations of top military officers.

Why do democratic societies perennially worry about their own military's periodic objections to civilian oversight and larger liberal values? Why, often in response, do military leaders conclude that they are either misunderstood or manipulated by civilian authorities whom they regard as naive or ignorant about military affairs?

IT IS A FACT WORTH REMEMBERING that the armed forces are inherently hierarchical organizations based on rank and the chain of command. There is no opportunity in military units for decision by majority vote when war begins. Once bullets fly, soldiers can ill afford to debate the wisdom of assaulting the next hill. They cannot worry about the "fairness" of a brilliant glib private having no influence in the decisions taken by an obtuse or blockheaded commanding officer.

Impatience, resolve, audacity—these necessary military traits are not necessarily those that democratic legislators and bureaucrats prize. Most politicians loathe a loud-mouthed George S. Patton in peacetime as much as they hunt out his swashbuckling style in time of war.

Sometimes the voting public suspects that professional soldiers like violence and killing, or at least far more than civilians do. And supposed sheep always worry about giving orders to hungry wolves. One needs only to read the sad letters of poor Cicero to see how in his arrogance he fatally misjudged entirely the military minds of an Augustus or Antony. Civilian overseers in France and later in Germany sought to solve emerging problems by dispatching Napoleon to Egypt or by throwing Hitler in jail but found that in the end these steps were but the beginning and not the end of their troubles. They had fatally misjudged these "troublemakers."

Then there is the ever-present fear of militarism—that is, the fear of the cult of arms that transcends the battlefield and becomes an ideology that celebrates power, rigid discipline, and fanatical devotion to a cause. Indeed, this exaggerated dimension of military life often draws the most zealous and dangerous of characters into its orbit. These can be truly scary folks, these Spartan *krypteia*, the Praetorian guards, or Hitler's SS. Such groups in the past have often interfered with or intervened in politics under the posture of being models of rigorous asceticism for the nation.

Anti-constitutional military coups, and not the idealistic promotion of democracy and liberal values, thus seem the more logical vice of military figures when they intrude into politics. History in some sense is the record of supposedly sober soldiers intervening in times of perceived social chaos to bring society a needed dose of their own order and obedience.

That was the rationale in 44 B.C. when Caesar crossed the Rubicon and put a formal end to the Roman Republic, Napoleon dismissed the Directorate, Hitler ended the Weimar Republic, and the twentieth-century Latin America caudillos, Greek colonels, and

Middle Eastern Baathist and Nasserite officers staged their various coups. Communist dictators in the Soviet Union and China inserted their own commissars into their militaries to ensure that they were perpetual advocates for Communist ideology and indoctrination, at home and abroad.

II. LIBERAL MILITARIES?

BUT THERE IS ANOTHER and less known tradition of what we might call "military liberalism" under which militaries have often given birth to or facilitated the creation of free governments and have been used in turn to promote and extend them abroad. The challenge facing the United States in the twenty-first century is not so much a rebellious military establishment or an endless Pentagon desire for adventurism overseas.

Given our overwhelming military superiority in the world, it is surprising that our military leaders are somewhat loath to exercise that power in aggressive ways, no doubt fearing they will be called upon to lead an endless cavalcade of humanitarian missions. The more intriguing challenge concerns the degree to which political authorities will use our armed forces in ways that reflect American values and political aims and to what degree our officers will be willing to carry out those objectives. The challenge, in other words, is for civilian authorities to build upon this other tradition—the tradition of military liberalism.

In fact, democracy has always been nearly synonymous with wars of national expression. Fifth-century B.C. Athens fought three out of four years in its greatest age of cultural achievement—usually goaded on by a vote of the assembly, usually to fight some sort of oligarch state. America since World War II has seen its troops in combat in, or in the skies above, Afghanistan, Bosnia, Cambodia, Cuba, the Dominican Republic, Grenada, Haiti, Iran, Iraq, Korea,

Kosovo, Kuwait, Lebanon, Libya, Panama, Serbia, Somalia, and Vietnam—all with the professed aim of restoring some sort of order by fighting oligarchs, dictators, and autocrats.

Consensual governments ratify wars, and thus rarely can the people successfully argue that they were forced into them by kings or dictators. The historian Herodotus—noting the propensity for democracies to be fickle and ready to fight for idealistic reasons— remarked that it was easier to persuade 30,000 Athenian citizens to send aid to the Ionia during the revolt from Persia than to convince a few Spartan oligarchs to do the same. It is hard to think of many democracies that were not born in some manner out of war, violence, or coercion—beginning with the first example of Cleisthenic Athens in 507 B.C., and including our own revolution in 1776. The best examples are the most recent of the twentieth century, when many of the most successful present-day constitutional governments were epiphenomena of war, imposed by the victors or coalition partners, as we have seen in the cases of Germany, Japan, Italy, South Korea, and more recently Grenada, Haiti, Liberia, Panama, Serbia—and Afghanistan and Iraq.

OF COURSE, DEMOCRACY, as Aristotle outlined its various wide parameters in the *Politics*, is in some sense a relative term. Scholars still argue over its definition—and especially the weight that should be given to the criteria for voting, the degree of constitutional rights granted to the individual, and the relationship of political freedom with concurrent economic and social liberty.

But if we adopt the most expansive sense of the notion of constitutional government, parliamentary Britain of the nineteenth century was far more consensual than nearly all nations of its own time and even our own. And British officers sometimes used their overwhelming military superiority to promote a classical sense of liberalism, whether in ending suttee in India or shutting down African slave trade.

We sometimes forget that the existential global evils of the nineteenth and twentieth centuries—chattel slavery, Nazism, Italian Fascism, Japanese militarism, and Soviet Stalinism—were not only eliminated by force or the threat of force, but exclusively by the might of democratically governed militaries. American armies or the threat of them ended the plantation system, the death camps, the Co-Prosperity Sphere, and the Gulag, and made possible the future of the new Atlanta, the new Tokyo, and the new Berlin alike. Even during Roman imperial times, when the first emperors succeeded in suppressing the autonomy of the Senate and central assemblies, there still functioned at the local level the concepts of Roman law that allowed all Roman citizens the same rights of habeas corpus, trial by a magistrate, and protections of private property. The armies of the late republic that swept the Mediterranean did not do so solely on the brilliant discipline, tactics, and technology of the legions. They also offered to the conquered the promise that Roman proconsuls and legates would use legionaries to enforce a sense of equality under the law for indigenous tribes from Gaul to North Africa—a reality that often undermined local nationalist resistance leaders.

It is not just governments *per se* that democratically inspired armies often protect and promote, but often the wider cultures that incubate and nurture them. And that allows them often to be more effective agents of change and custodians of more liberal values. The present-day Turkish armed forces, at last subject to elected officials and the products of military science and professional training, still adhere to the secular statutes that Kemal Ataturk established for the entire country. The military is thus paradoxically the essential guardian of liberal values in that country, the one institution that is most likely to resist the insidious imposition of Sharia law or the Islamization of Turkish culture.

Racial integration and gender equality were much easier achieved in the U.S. military than in civilian institutions, once reformist politicians discovered that the military's chain of command and culture

159

of obedience could be used much more efficiently to impose democratic agendas from on high.

The armed forces of the democracies like fifth-century B.C. Athens, fourth-century B.C. Thebes, or contemporary America all tried to promote abroad not just the values that they cherished at home, but often to replicate their own democratic structures abroad. Why should this be so?

III. DEMOCRACY AND MILITARY SELF-INTEREST

THE ANSWER IS COMPLEX but seems to involve both practical and ethical reasons in seeing as many democracies as possible spread beyond their own shores. The so-called *ochlos* at Athens—the voting mob empowered by the radical democracy—felt that its own privileged position hinged on having like-minded supporters in the subject states of the Aegean. The maritime Athenian empire was patrolled by two hundred imperial triremes with names like "Free Speech" and "Demokratia," and powered by poor landless *thete* rowers who were paid a generous wage as the muscles of democracy. The truism that democracies rarely attack each other is mostly valid in the modern era and perhaps for antiquity as well. Although democratic Athens attacked democratic Syracuse during the Peloponnesian War, such internecine warfare among democratic polities was not the norm. The historian Thucydides saw that the Peloponnesian War pitted the Athenians democratic allies and subjects mostly against the oligarchies aligned with Sparta. He also observed that Athenian forces did not fight so well against the Sicilians when it was thought that Sicily had something in common with Athenian political culture.

National security was also at least part of the catalyst for the great march of Epaminondas the Theban in 369 B.C. Then the general took a huge democratic army down into the Peloponnese to end the Spartan land empire, free the Messenian helot serfs, and found the democratic citadels at Mantineia, Megalopolis, and Messene in order to encircle Sparta. After all that, Sparta never again marched north of the Isthmus at Corinth—a routine occurrence before Epaminondas' invasion.

The European Union apparently has achieved its promised anomaly of a continent of autonomous states that will not attack one another—a dream made feasible only by the institutionalization of democracy made possible by the allied victory and democratization after World War II, and the collapse of the Soviet Union after its defeat in the Cold War.

Democratic militaries are also imbued with moral logic that there is an inherent ethical inconsistency in protecting democracy at home while undermining it abroad. One of the raging controversies of the Cold War was the criticism that the United States had somehow birthed, often armed, or occasionally supported a rogue's gallery of dictators like Ferdinand Marcos, Georgios Papadopoulos, Augusto Pinochet, the Shah of Iran, and Anastasio Somoza—and that this cynicism was a betrayal of American values. The post-Cold War hope was that the *Realpolitik* that marked U.S. policy during that era was an aberration of sorts, owing to the emergence of the Soviet Union as a nuclear power with expansionist ambitions. The collapse of the Soviet empire thus created the conditions for a new emphasis in U.S. foreign policy. Accordingly, the American intervention in Panama, the 1991 Gulf War, the bombing of Kosovo and Serbia, and the wars in Afghanistan and Iraq (whatever the underlying wisdom or folly of those interventions) were aimed at dictators with the expectation that their removal would be followed by the imposition of democratic rule.

IV. DREAMS AND REALITIES AFTER THE COLD WAR

WHEN GEORGE BUSH senior did not push reform on Iraq or the region as a whole after the defeat of Saddam Hussein in 1991, critics at home alleged that such realism was no longer appropriate in the post-Cold War world. The public, it seemed, was appalled at Secretary of State James Baker's declaration that the war in the oil-rich area was to be fought solely over "jobs, jobs, jobs" and, later, that a successful war had only led to years of no-fly zones to prevent continual butchery of the Shiites and Kurds.

Indeed, one of the ironies of the present round of attacks on George W. Bush's Iraqi war—too much emphasis on democracy, not enough troops, too much confidence in Iraqi reformers, too little fear of Iran, an international coalition that was too small—is that it was advanced by authors and writers like Michael Gordon, Thomas Ricks, Bernard Trainor, Bob Woodward, and others who in the 1990s had critiqued the first Gulf War in books and articles on nearly opposite grounds: that it was not fought with sufficient idealism, that too many troops were deployed, that too little confidence was placed in Shiite and Kurdish reformers, that the fighting coalition was too large and unwieldy, that the strategists had excessive fear of Iran.

As Robert Kagan notes in his recent book *Dangerous Nation* (a history of American intervention abroad), democracies that profess egalitarianism and the freedom of the individual are especially sensitive to charges of cynicism and hypocrisy when their foreign policies do not reflect their own values. At worst the United States fought its covert, dirty wars on the basis of economic or strategic pragmatism, which meant that it was quite willing to install compliant thugs whom it felt might be better than the alternative and might in time evolve into something more liberal. But in its more conventional conflicts that were closely covered by the press and followed by the public on a daily basis (World Wars I and II, Korea, Vietnam, and the contemporary Middle East conflicts), U.S. administrations generally sought to implant constitutional governments in postwar landscapes without delay.

It would thus appear that, to the degree the military has an active consultative role in picking and choosing America's fights, it would not oppose but might indeed support the concept of promoting democracy as an expression of the national interest. Nor does the broader public oppose such a role for our military. Even in controversial cases like Iraq and Afghanistan, the public is strongly supportive of military efforts to birth consensual government in the wake of the removal of dictators, notwithstanding the difficulties of doing so. Most Americans understand that the alternative—restoring order by imposing a friendly strongman—would only sharpen the charge of cynical colonialism, imperialism, and corporatism. If it is true that the spread of democracy around the world will make wars less likely and less frequent, then the military might see democratization as a means of reducing the likelihood of its own deployment in dangerous foreign wars to come.

As a consequence, for a full generation now the all-volunteer American military has trained an entire cadre of officers who have received advanced degrees in our finest academic institutions and thus possess proconsul skills that far exceed those necessary to command men in battle. "Winning hearts and minds" is now deemed just as important to the training of military officers as mastering GPS bombing techniques or the proper uses of the Abrams tank.

The theme of Robert Kaplan's *Imperial Grunts* was that in far-off diverse areas such as Colombia, Mongolia, and the Philippines, the U.S. military is not only conducting counter-insurgency warfare in "Injun Country," but training local troops to operate under constitutional government. Special Forces officers administer to the social and economic needs of local constituents for the purpose of stabilizing local governments so that they will not exploit discontent or use oil or drug revenues to destabilize the global order that has grown up since World War II. The United States, obviously, has a vital interest in defending and extending this order that promises to extend the sphere of prosperity and democracy.

IN THE FUROR OVER THE WAR IN IRAQ, however, the entire notion of "nation-building" both in small backwaters and at the conclusion of major military interventions—relatively unquestioned after Panama, the Balkans, and Afghanistan—is now under intense scrutiny and re-examination. The post-Iraq foreign policy of the United States, to the extent it is not isolationist, will probably see calls for the return of a posture of cynical realism, meaning that we should accept the fact that we have to make arrangements with the world as it is rather than trying to change it in our own image. This might involve the acceptance of an attitude of "more rubble, less trouble" leading to a strategy of stand-off bombing to deal with trouble spots in the world. Or yet again, future administrations will accept de facto appeasement of those who threaten our security in the hope that they will go away or their anger will thereby be assuaged. This we have already seen in the policy that terrorism warrants only an occasional cruise missile or, as a criminal justice matter, a federal indictment. All of these approaches might be tried as alternatives to "nation-building" or "democratization."

Richard Haass, president of the Council on Foreign Relations, remarked in a recent interview, "We're discovering that the conventional military power for which the United States is best known is most relevant to classic battlefields like the first Iraq war [in 1991], but the struggles we're engaged in now and for the foreseeable future are anything but classic." Haass adds that battling guerrilla insurgencies and salvaging failing states such as Iraq and Afghanistan with nation-building are not skills at which the U.S. government has excelled. "So we're finding it very hard to translate classic military superiority into stability in these struggles."

In summing up the pessimism that swept New York and Washington during 2007, Haass grandly concluded, "For a number of reasons, I believe we are entering an era where U.S. power and relative influence, in the Middle East especially, is reduced and the influence of others who have anything but a pro-American outlook is increasing, and that trend is likely to continue for decades to come. I predict this realignment will be enduring."

This gloom is now shared by thinkers as diverse as Niall Ferguson and Francis Fukuyama who in the fumes of Iraq see only perils in promoting democratization. They understand that such idealism is best in tune with our own values. And they concede it has worked

164

in the past after other victories. But their concern centers mostly on the practicality rather than the desirability of such a stance in today's more chaotic and globalized world.

Freed from the distortions of the Cold War, and after a decade of using our military to promote democracy through the use of arms, has the idea of "military liberalism" run aground in Iraq? And if so, why?

V. WHAT WENT WRONG?

FIRST THE UNITED STATES put the cart of postwar reconstruction ahead of the proverbial horse of defeating—and humiliating—the enemy. In this regard, in present and future wars of the twenty-first century we are faced with two mutually exclusive propositions. In an era of globalized communications, and of a therapeutic rather than tragic mindset on the part of Western elites, it is very difficult to bring wars to their full conclusions—that is, to defeat the enemy and humiliate him to such a degree that he submits to the dictates of peace.

In an age of multiculturalism, moral equivalence, and utopian pacifism, the carnage necessary to disabuse the enemy of continuing in his present course is often seen as immoral, counterproductive, or unnecessary. Most strategic thinkers thought our pullback in Fallujah, Iraq, in the spring of 2004 was a costly mistake—a half-measure that necessitated a belated reentry by the post-election autumn. Then after renewed fighting to take the town, which was far bloodier than the initial conflict, our soldiers found torture cells, bomb factories, and a veritable terropolis that had been constructed after our withdrawal.

But almost the opposite reaction to that siege seems true in Western popular culture. Compare a play running in spring 2007 in London called *Fallujah* by Jonathan Holmes, highlighting American atrocities inflicted on the insurgents in 2004. Lest one think that the play's criticism of the U.S military is simply vintage far-left rhetoric, consider the review by the supposedly staid *Economist* of what it conceded was an "anti-war, anti-American" drama:

> The audience shuffles about his landscape while the action takes place around them. Soldiers push their way through, swaggering and malevolent; a roving stage light suddenly picks out two women in the audience as Iraqi aid workers. They weave gracefully through the crowd, telling their story, placing a hand gently on someone's shoulder.

Again, lest one thinks that this is a fair and descriptive (rather than an opinionated) view by a British status quo magazine, consider the *Economist*'s final assessment that follows disclaimers of the play's obvious bias: "*Fallujah* can still be applauded for casting light on a shameful chapter in a disastrous war."

"Shameful" and "disastrous"? This cheap sermonizing of Western elites reflects two unspoken truths: Privately, no well-heeled British subject would prefer the world of beheading, gender apartheid, and Sharia law that flourished in lawless Fallujah to the legal system and audit that governs the American military. And yet most elites understand in the present age, that their own professional advancement, psychological well-being, and political acceptance come from criticizing the U.S. Armed Forces. Thus the war to establish democracy to replace Saddam Hussein's genocidal rule must be reduced to "swaggering Americans" threatening female "Iraqi aid workers."

IN FEAR OF TELEVISED COLLATERAL civilian damage, in worry over taking casualties, and sensitive to anti-war sentiment at home, it is no wonder that the American military is reluctant to annihilate its enemies. It did not do so in Gulf War I. The televised scenes alone on the so-called "Highway of Death" helped to call off that bombing of fleeing Iraqi soldiers who had committed outrages in Kuwait and were quite prepared to do even worse to the Kurds and Shiites when given a reprieve.

The dragging of naked American corpses in the streets of Mogadishu ended President Clinton's humanitarian efforts in Somalia. And after 3,400 dead in Iraq, the narrative is the IED and suicide vest, not the purple finger of democratic participants. At home the rhetoric of Cindy Sheehan, Michael Moore, and former President Jimmy Carter has reduced George Bush to a demonic figure, and our efforts in Iraq to a war for oil, a proxy war for Israel, or a profit-making enterprise on behalf of Halliburton. Gone from the script is the remembrance that roughly the same number of Americans was killed on September 11 by Islamic terrorists, or that this country in its various wars of the past has on occasion suffered more casualties in a week than we have in four years in Iraq.

How odd that a war purportedly for oil saw the price of petroleum skyrocket. An extra half-trillion dollars in petrodollars annually flowed into the Middle East, and Iraqi oil concessions for the first time in thirty years have become transparent and adjudicated by popular government. How odd also that in the six years following September 11, the United States attacked just two governments, the Middle East's worst in the Taliban and Saddam Hussein, and yet was defamed for waging a unilateral and pre-emptive war as part of a neoconservative crusade to knock off one by one scores of unattractive dictatorships and implant democracy after democracy in their wake.

The point is that in the face of such criticism, the military apparently cannot inflict a level of hurt upon an enemy, or suffer a level of casualties, that in the past were deemed critical for victory and hence postwar stability and reconstruction. Saddam Hussein's Baathist army might have evaporated in April 2003. Yet its shamed officers and conscripts soon learned that a good way to restore Arab pride after such televised humiliation was to go home, strip off their uniforms, and reinvent themselves as patriotic insurgents.

Then the odds of safely killing, through remotely detonated IEDs, an American stringing telephone wires or painting a schoolhouse were far better than in the recent past when meeting him in a gun battle meant that outright war, not a CNN-televised "peace," governed the rules of engagement.

What worked in the Balkans in 1998, contrary to popular consensus, was not "multilateralism." The Clinton administration neither asked the U.S. Congress for approval nor even approached the United Nations. It had allowed NATO forces to languish on the sidelines watching a ten-year holocaust that took a quarter-million lives. Instead the key to eventual success was that a liberal American president was able to use the United States Air Force, in safety thousands of feet above in the skies over Serbia, to drop its new precision munitions on the very capital of a right-wing Christian European dictatorship without sacrificing a single American life.

BUT THE STARS SELDOM LINE UP so perfectly. Our wars to come will often have to be waged by conservative administrations against enemies in the former Third World—sometimes of different religions and colors than our own—and on the ground in messy primordial failed states, far from Europe.

A second worry is not so much military, as the *postbellum* practicality of extending democracy to traditional, non-Western societies that have little or no experience with ideas like liberty, equal rights, the rule of law, or representative government. Volumes have been written on the prerequisites—economic, social, cultural, and psychological—necessary for democratization.

I once argued in *The Other Greeks* that Athenian democracy—the West's first—was an epiphenomenon, impossible without two centuries of prior limited consensual government that first saw the establishment of rights of property-holding and inheritance and a solid middle class (the *mesoi*) of free-holding citizen-hoplite farmers. Then, and only then, was it possible to put into place the key attributes that we associate with Athenian democracy, such as the principle of one man, one vote and full political participation without regard to wealth.

The contemporary enigma in the Middle East, however, revolves around the question of to what degree globalization—the intrusion into traditional tribal life by television, DVDs, the Internet, and cell phones, along with the large numbers of contemporary democracies in the world at large—has collapsed the window of preparation necessary for reform. And while Islam, for example, seems not incompatible with democracy *per se* in countries like India, Indonesia, Malaysia, and Turkey (where over half the world's Muslims live), the Arab Islamic world may prove to be a different story altogether.

There the obstacles to democracy and Western ideals of liberty and equality seem more profound than elsewhere. These include a deeply entrenched tribal culture, endemic anger at modernity combined with a desire for the fruits of modernity, feelings of pan-Arabic chauvinism nursed on transnational solidarity, scapegoating of foreigners and foreign influences, intense feelings of grievance over a purportedly grand past juxtaposed to a miserable present, and dislocations brought about by the huge wealth of exporting a third of the world's daily petroleum consumption. All have combined to produce the anti-liberal practices and attitudes that are prevalent in the region: fundamentalism, terrorism, and a kind of nihilistic violence against any foreign influence, however well meaning or constructive it might be.

In other words, it is redundant now to advocate democratization in the regions of the world where it is easiest to promote or is already under way—eastern Europe or a prosperous capitalistic Asia especially. When we talk of nation-building in the future, it will almost always be in the context of the Middle East where there is uniform autocracy, plenty of petroleum, radical Islamism, terrorism, promises to annihilate Israel, and soon nuclear-tipped missiles.

VI. A FUTURE FOR NATION-BUILDING?

SO WHERE DOES THIS ALL LEAVE US? We need no more banal lectures about the truth we all know: mere plebiscites are not democracy; such desirable government emerges ideally in concert with some sort of institutionalization of human rights, transparency, a free press, and an independent judiciary; and war and democratization should not be preemptory, but the last resorts taken only when such idealism is first subservient to our national survival.

We all know that—and also know that such "wisdom" doesn't offer much guidance in a world not of our own choosing. The future for the West at war is one of poor choices. The worst is to allow anti-Western dictators to murder at will; then there is the bad alternative of trying to thwart them by encouraging democratic reforms under nearly impossible conditions.

After the hysteria over Iraq begins to subside, we may all wish to be Jacksonians—muscular isolationists who are tired of past unappreciated sacrifice and thus willing to act unilaterally and punitively, but only when it is deemed directly necessary to our own immediate survival.

Yet it will not be so easy to quite close the book on neoconservatism and resurrect George W. Bush's 2000 campaign promise not to use the American military for "nation building." First, we must remember that realism—whether pampering the House of Saud or offering encouragement to Pakistani "President" Musharraf—has been tried before and did nothing to circumvent either the attacks of September 11 or nuclear proliferation. Both autocracies—Saudi and Pakistani—stealthily continue to either fund or offer sanctuary to al Qaeda terrorists. Nor did appeasement prove successful, as we are reminded by those often cited two-decade-long serial assaults from the Tehran hostage-taking of 1979 to the 2000 attack on the USS *Cole*.

Second, nation-building as a reaction to a foreign threat is both familiar to the American experience and reflects the values and aspirations of the United States. The postwar world as we know it exists only because the United States fostered democracy in Europe, Japan, and Korea. That has not changed, and will not change.

But what has changed today is not so much our policies or goals, but in the cauldron of Iraq and Afghanistan, it is we ourselves who have changed to the point that we have lost the confidence to enact positive reform abroad *at a price in blood and treasure deemed worth the effort.*

It matters little that our present aspirations are far less grandiose in Iraq, and our losses far fewer, than were true in democratizing Germany, Italy, Japan, or Korea. The key, instead, is only our current perceptions of what constitutes a foreign endeavor that is too costly or painful to endure. In our era of postmodernism and globalism, the challenge is not so much to use the American military to thwart autocracies and help foster constitutional government in their place, as to convince the American people that we have little choice—and that we have done so in the past with success, and can do so again in the future.

In short, our present wars are harder to bring to their full completion. The nature of our defeated enemies makes it far more difficult to democratize them. Western democratic publics are far more reluctant to spend even a fraction of the blood and treasure that were needed to rebuild Europe and Japan into successful democratic societies. The future is not more of Afghanistan and Iraq, but more Rwandas and Darfurs, where the rhetoric of idealism increases even as our willingness to use our military to enact desirable reform erodes.

(July/August 2007)

Victory Is the Only Option

Andrew Roberts

Andrew Roberts reminds us that the Anglo-American partnership has proved vital over the past century in defense of the West and its heritage of free institutions. Disagreements over the war in Iraq may have frayed this relationship, but they must not be permitted to undermine it altogether. As Mr. Roberts argues, America's defense of liberty against the forces of a new Dark Age will require a return to the traditional friendships and commitments that allowed her to prevail in every civilizational showdown since 1900.

"CAN THE IDEALS THAT MADE AMERICA GREAT Provide a Model for the World?" That was the question that the editors of *The American Spectator* posed to ten of the most sagacious thinkers of the Western world, under the overall title: "The Pursuit of Liberty." The ten answers have been wise, thought-provoking, and essential reading for anybody concerned with this most fundamental issue of our time.

For will the ideals of 1776—those that have so far actuated the most powerful nation in the history of mankind—survive and prosper in the next stage of our global story, or might we be truly heading for a new Dark Age? Could it be that today the combined forces of Islamic fundamentalist totalitarianism, Chinese neo-Communism, European anti-Americanism, rogue state nihilism, neutral state indifference, and—by far the most dangerous of all—our own doubts and disbelief in what we stand for, mean the slow eclipse of Western civilization? Might Barbarism finally triumph over Learning, Law, and Light?

In 1940 Winston Churchill warned of the way that the world would "sink into the abyss of a new Dark Age" if the Axis powers won the Second World War. The danger is no less great today should the ideals that inspire the English-speaking peoples and their allies be defeated in the present War on Terror. *The American Spectator* and the estimable John Templeton Foundation deserve credit for their foresight in bringing together ten of our most distinguished commentators to discuss this central question of our age.

The left regularly denounces its opponents for being "knee-jerk," "unthinking," even "Neanderthal" right-wingers, thus assuming an intellectual superiority that on closer examination is utterly baseless. What better response than to publish the views of ten intellectuals who—although by no means are all on the political right—certainly do not conform to the left's prescription for the future of the West, the politics of the pre-emptive cringe. Instead, this essay series is the written equivalent of the kind of lecture program that one would have loved to have attended at university, and at which there would have been standing room only.

THE SERIES BEGAN IN SEPTEMBER 2006 with "American Exceptionalism" by James Q. Wilson, the Ronald Reagan Professor of Public Policy at Pepperdine University. Charting the ways in which the United States was profoundly historically different from any other country in the world, Wilson was nonetheless highly cautious about the extent to which her values could be successfully exported to the rest of the world, largely because she also exported, "to no collective applause, blue jeans, Big Macs, rock and hip-hop music, web-based pornography, and motion pictures that often celebrate violence and a shallow adolescent culture." It was a thoughtful and sobering start to the series.

Next came "America's Democratization Projects Abroad" by James Kurth, a senior fellow at Philadelphia's renowned Foreign Policy Research Institute and the editor of its excellent journal, *Orbis*. Looking back over the century since Woodrow Wilson tried "to make the world safe for democracy," Kurth saw some fine successes—Germany, Italy, and Japan post-WWII foremost among them—but foresaw serious danger were democratic elections in the Middle East and the Muslim world to bring Islamofascist governments to power. He also wondered whether democracy in China might not unleash centrifugal tendencies and secessionism, rather than enlightenment and liberty.

Norman Podhoretz hailed President George W. Bush's Second Inaugural Address as "A Masterpiece of American Oratory" in the November issue, describing it as a speech that was "wildly misunderstood." Likening it to inaugural addresses from Truman, Kennedy, and even Lincoln, Podhoretz made a powerful case for Bush's central argument, that American "vital interests and our deepest beliefs are now one," and that advancing the ideals that "created our nation" is "the calling of our time."

Lawrence E. Harrison of Tufts University then addressed the cultural dimension of political, social, and economic development, which he argued persuasively, had been too long ignored because of its necessarily subjective nature. Because culture cannot be quantified in the precise way that electoral votes, troop movements, welfare budgets, and cash transfers can be, it has tended to have been left out of the equation, yet the cultural aspect of the present struggle was vital for the success of liberty.

Daniel Johnson, one of Britain's foremost conservative intellectuals, went one stage further. In perhaps the most passionate of all the essays, he argued that Europe ignored the increasing Islamicization of its large immigrant Muslim communities at its peril. Noting that the anti-American "rot set in" during the Cold War, when

Europe for the first time failed to finance its own arms expenditure, Johnson also pointed out how post-imperial "disenchantment lies at the heart of Europe's self-absorption." America's hopes and fears should be Europe's too, he contended, and if Europeans refuse to support President Bush in his attempt "to halt the Islamo-Nazis in their tracks, then Europeans will have proved themselves unworthy of their ancestors at Thermopylae and Marathon." In this powerful essay as in much else of his writing, Johnson laid claim to his father Paul's mantle as being a modern-day seer.

Johnson's philippic was followed in the April edition by "Liberty for Strangers: American Power and the Predicament for Arabs," an equally sagacious contribution from Fouad Ajami of the Johns Hopkins University School of Advanced International Studies. He approached the issue from the Arab perspective, pointing out how popular were Fascist and Nazi ideas in the Middle East in the late 1930s and early 1940s. He also highlighted the central paradox that American liberals, who for so long had stood for liberty, now felt "it was a fool's errand to take liberty to strangers," whereas it fell to a conservative Republican president to try to do the right thing by the Middle East.

Natan Sharansky and Ron Dermer, who in 2004 co-authored the hugely influential book *The Case for Democracy*, emphasized the horrors that could lie ahead were the United States simply to turn its back on Iraq, and thereby "hand the enemies of freedom a great victory." Of course, all non-democratic states in the world actively want the U.S. to be defeated in Iraq, because the days of their own repression will be numbered if she is victorious and democracy prospers there and subsequently elsewhere too. "Democracy in Iraq is possible," the authors stated with commendable faith, "because so many Iraqis want to be free and because the leader of the free world has not abandoned them to face the enemies of freedom alone."

Michael Novak agreed in the June issue, arguing, "Against tremendous ridicule, abuse, and sheer visceral hatred from his political foes and significant elements in the press, the President had to remain as hard and firm as a diamond-tipped drill." This leading intellectual light of the American Enterprise Institute was certain that "America's effort to promote freedom in the world and protect her own security from Islamic extremism is ultimately dependent on success in Iraq." Although Novak feared that the 21,500 extra U.S. troops deployed in the spring and summer 2007 surge might be "too little, too late," nonetheless he believes that the success or failure of the democratic experiment in Iraq is of world-historical importance.

The tenth and final one of these fascinating, thought-provoking, and valuable essays appeared in the last issue, where Victor Davis Hanson, a senior fellow at the Hoover Institution, wrote about the past, present, and future "Armies for Democracy." His profoundly depressing, but possibly accurate, thesis is that the United States had simply "lost the confidence to enact positive reform abroad at a price in blood and treasure deemed worth the effort."

Although, as Hanson persuasively argues, that price is a mere fraction of the price that America has been willing to pay several times before in her recent history, he points out that today it is American willpower that is lacking, rather than any other commodity. (Certainly as a Briton, I only wish your 1776 Congress had contained as many Murthas, Obamas, and Pelosis as your present one does: George Washington would not have stood a chance in his long, drawn-out, and desperate struggle against my countrymen.)

THE ESSAY SERIES THUS ENDED on a sobering note, after contributions from ten of the most acute thinkers of our day, each of them passionately committed to the defense of Western civilization. As a coda to their thoughts, I would like to present my own contribution to the debate, and try to encourage Americans to see their present world-historical War on Terror through the prism of the three earlier struggles of the English-speaking peoples and their allies since 1900.

Less than two weeks before he died, Theodore Roosevelt wrote to Rudyard Kipling, saying that "I have always insisted that the really good understanding the British Empire and the United States would not come except insofar as we developed a thoroughly American type, separate from every European type and free alike from mean antipathy and mean cringing." He denied the claims of "the [Woodrow] Wilson adherents and the Sinn Feiners and pro-Germans and Socialists and Pacifists" that he was a craven Anglophile. However, he did add: "Because of the almost identity of the written (as opposed to the spoken) language and from other reasons I think that on the whole, and when there isn't too much gush and effusion and too much effort to bring them together, the people of our two countries are naturally closer than those of any others."

Roosevelt intensely deprecated the "good, mushy, well-meaning creatures who are always striving to bring masses of Englishmen and Americans together," and likened them to a philanthropist he once knew who was saddened by the historic antipathy between New York's police and fire departments. In order for them to "get together," this rich man had hired Yankee Stadium for a friendly game of baseball. The moment the umpire's decision was disputed in the opening innings, Roosevelt recalled, both sides did indeed "get together," in a vast brawl with hundreds of "stalwart men in uniform" exchanging blows with each other.

If relations between the United States and Great Britain have managed on the whole to avoid Roosevelt's Yankee Stadium metaphor, it has largely been because of the threats that they have faced together and the comity between successive pairs of presidents and premiers who have together fought against them. Although they never met, Lord Salisbury and Theodore Roosevelt established a fine working relationship that saw both countries through the potential strains of the Spanish-American and Boer Wars. Similarly, the warm personal relationships between Franklin D. Roosevelt and Winston Churchill, Ronald Reagan and Margaret Thatcher, and George W. Bush and Tony Blair have reminded us of what the English-speaking peoples can together achieve for civilization. (Equally, their two great twentieth-century defeats of Suez and Vietnam both took place when Britain and America were not "standing shoulder to shoulder.")

THE WORLD TODAY is facing the fourth great Fascist threat since 1900, one that can only be defeated if Anglo-American amity is kept in as good repair as it was by those earlier statesman-paladins. The proto-Fascist threat posed by Prussian militarism in 1914–18 was ended in part by the eruption onto the Western Front of General Pershing's million-man "doughboy" army, just as it was most needed to help turn back Hindenburg and Ludendorff's great Spring Offensive of 1918. Similarly, Axis Fascism was destroyed in great part by carrying through the masterly "Germany First" decision arrived at in the Anglo-American Arcadia Conference in Washington of December 1941–January 1942. So also did Soviet "Red Fascism" meet its end after the economic life-blood was squeezed out of it during the Glorious Eighties. These were not quick or easy victories, and neither will the next one be in the latest mutation of Fascism that we presently face. Although victory is not yet in sight, knowing what we do of the fundamentalist fanaticism that drives Islamofascism, such a victory is utterly indispensable.

The Great War took four years to win, World War II six, the Cold War forty-four. At this exponential rate, the War on Terror might take much longer. Liberal sneers that President Bush misnamed the war "because you can't fight against an abstract noun" are misapplied; "[Wilhelmine] militarism," "[Axis] aggression," and "[Soviet] Communism" are all grammatically abstract, yet were all brought to heel in their time. Pentagon officials are right to be calling this one "The Long War." As a recent *New York Times* article was headlined: "Blair, in Kabul, Warns That Fight Against the Taliban Will Take Decades." In his speech Blair pointed out how: "Here, in this extraordinary piece of desert, is where the future of world security in the early twenty-first century is going to be played out." As so very often in his foreign policy pronouncements since 9/11, the prime minister was tough, forthright, brave, and—most importantly—right.

When one surveys the forces serving in Afghanistan, beyond the steadily improving Afghan army itself, one sees 15,500 Americans, 5,500 Britons, 3,500 Canadians, 550 Australians, and important special forces contingents from New Zealand. Meanwhile, one sees Germany confining its troops to the quiet north, France to guard duty on the Khyber Pass, and other NATO nations refusing to contribute more reinforcements to what is surely the most morally justifiable war in recent history—fought against the movement that hosted and protected al Qaeda up to 9/11. Once again, therefore, it is the English-speaking peoples who find themselves in the forefront of protecting civilization. As NATO approaches the beginning of the end of its natural life, torn apart by European refusals to play a big enough military, political, financial, or moral role in the War on Terror, the USA should be increasingly looking to the English-speaking peoples for camaraderie, mutual support, and shared ideals.

For it is not simply Britain and America that deserve plaudits for defeating the great Fascist threats of the past and standing up doughtily against the present danger. The contributions of the rest of the English-speaking peoples—except sadly Ireland—have also been considerable over the 107 years since 1900. The statistics are astonishing, and in some cases make the pure Anglo-American ones pall by comparison. For example, over 100,000 New Zealanders served during the Great War, from a country with a total population of only 1.1 million in 1914.

A young and numerically tiny country, with a 1914 population of only four million, Australia lost no fewer than 58,961 killed in the Great War and 166,811 wounded—an enormous and terrible contribution to victory. In all, 416,809 Australians enlisted for service in the First World War, representing 38.7 percent of the total male population aged between eighteen and forty-four.

Canada's contribution to victory in the Second World War was incredible considering her population of only eleven million. In the spring of 1939 there were 10,000 men in her armed forces; by the end of the war, over one million had served in them. In the meantime they had been, in Professor David Dilks's words, "the only properly organized, trained and equipped military strength in the southern part of England in the perilous summer of autumn of 1940" and had fought in Hong Kong in Christmas 1941, as well as at Dieppe, Sicily, Italy, France, and the Low Countries. The Royal Canadian Navy had 500 ships in service by 1943, and was the third-largest navy in the world by 1945. No fewer than 125,000 Commonwealth aircrew were trained in Canada, and of the RAF's 487 squadrons in 1944, 100 came from the Dominions.

Nor was this an Anglo-Saxon racial phenomenon. By November 1918 no fewer than 15,204 Caribbean men had served in the eleven battalions of the British West Indies Regiment, which saw service in Palestine, Egypt, Mesopotamia, East Africa, India, France, Italy, Belgium, and England. "They were subjected to enemy artillery bombardment, sniper fire, exploding ammunition dumps and aerial attacks," records their historian. "In France, life was also made uncomfortable by the prevalence of fleas, lice and rats, while in Egypt there were problems with scorpions, lizards, snakes and especially flies. Nevertheless, in every theater the West Indians consistently displayed courage and discipline." Their decorations included no fewer than nineteen Military Crosses, eleven Military Crosses with bar, thirty-seven Military Medals, eleven Military Medals with Bar, forty-nine mentions in dispatches, eleven Medailles d'Honneur, and fourteen Royal Human Society's Medals, a proud total for any unit.

THE CRITICISM DIRECTED by the left-liberal media on both sides of the Atlantic against Messrs. Bush and Blair is of course nothing new in the conflicts of the English-speaking peoples. "There is a cowardly imbecile at the head of the government," warned one newspaper. "I am heartsick," cried one member of Congress, "at the mismanagement of the Army." And, "disgust with our government is universal," said another critic. That quote comes from historian Jay Winik's excellent recent book *April 1865*, recording some of the very modern-sounding criticisms leveled against Abraham Lincoln during the latter stages of the American Civil War.

The determined opposition of the left-liberal intelligentsia to the War on Terror, which due to its cultural hegemony has sadly seeped into the consciousness of the English-speaking peoples, has somehow led to a situation in which perhaps a majority of the electorates of every constituent nation (except doughty Australia) is willing to consider "defeat as an option" in Iraq. Of course, if we allow the notion to be bruited abroad that the only wars the English-speaking peoples could ever fight are those that have had a priori approval of NBC, CBS, CNN, the BBC, the *Washington Post, New York Times, Guardian,* and *Independent*, then their World Hegemon status might as well just be turned over to China right now, all wrapped up with big red satin bows decorating it.

Furthermore, defeat in the War on Terror means that the Iraqis and Afghans who are presently putting their trust in the English-speaking peoples will be massacred. They will therefore join a long line of people, including the South Vietnamese, Kurds, and Iraqi Marsh Arabs who were first encouraged by the West, only to be left to their own defenses afterwards. Americans need only visit Degas's monumental painting "The Execution of Maximilian" in New York's Museum of Modern Art to see the fate awaiting premier al-Maliki and his colleagues once the West withdraws its troops—as Napoleon III withdrew his from the protection of the hapless Emperor of Mexico—and they try to struggle on against the revolutionaries. The U.S. Congress has let down so many of America's friends and clients since the humiliating scenes on the roof of the Saigon embassy in 1975. We must not see any repeat of that.

ALTHOUGH EACH INDIVIDUAL DEATH of Coalition servicemen in the War on Terror is a tragedy for their loved ones, the numbers must be seen in an overall military, historical, and demographic context. At the time of writing, the United States has lost just 3,555 killed and Great Britain has lost 153. In 2006, the United States topped

300 million in total population, so the numbers killed fighting the Taliban and al Qaeda represent 0.1 percent of her population. Put another way, as many U.S. Marines died taking the single Japanese-held island of Tarawa in three weeks than U.S. soldiers in all the services have died in more than four years fighting in the Middle East, against fanatics who loathe America just as much as any kamikaze pilot.

Once one strips away the friendly fire incidents and other accidents, the number of British servicemen dying per year since 2003 has not been wildly out of kilter with the annual numbers of those murdered by the IRA. Furthermore, 153 killed represents the death toll of a very quiet weekend during the Western Front in the Great War. If one takes into account the vast numbers of U.S. servicemen who have served in Iraq over the past four years, multiplying the number of men by the number of missions they have undertaken, the death toll is astonishing low and a tribute to the troops' professionalism and their officers' leadership. This is not something any politician can point out, but by historical terms the Bush administration has overthrown a tyrant and installed a democracy at relatively low cost in American lives. Furthermore, there have been no terrorist outrages on the American homeland in the nearly six years since 9/11, something few would have foreseen that terrible day.

Similarly, once one dismisses with contumely the absurd figures bandied about by people such as the (anti-war) editor of the *Lancet* as to the number of Iraqis killed, the likely number of fewer than 150,000 pales into near-insignificance beside the death tolls of at least a dozen post-1945 conflicts in Africa and Asia, where over one million people have perished. In world history, context is all. Only by putting our losses—heart-wrenchingly sad though each individual one of course is—into a proper overall historical perspective, can one appreciate that this war is simply not "another Vietnam," where total U.S. losses exceeded 58,000 killed, or another Korea.

(Of course Iraq is not "another Vietnam" for any number of other reasons also, including type of terrain, status of enemy, support from

Great Powers, and possibility of final negotiated settlement. The Viet Cong were supported by the majority of the North Vietnamese in a way that is simply not the case with the Iraqis and the jihadists today. Were Hanoi capable of unleashing a dirty bomb in downtown Manhattan, it is doubtful it would have done so; with al Qaeda there can be no question that it would. The similarity between the conflicts instead lies with us, not our enemy, specifically in the U.S. Congress's willingness to quit the struggle once the network evening news programs started doling out a nightly diet of negative stories about the conflict.)

TO HAVE PURSUED a War on Terror in which the English-speaking peoples' most outspoken foe—and Terrorism's most active friend—was allowed to walk free would have been a political, military, and diplomatic absurdity. There was a superb case to be made for the overthrow of Saddam Hussein that mentioned neither the United Nations Resolutions, nor Weapons of Mass Destruction, nor even his despicable human rights record, and it is a shame that in the cacophony over WMDs it was not considered more thoroughly, for it is one that is largely immune from left-liberal criticism.

Saddam was responsible for many attempts to shoot down RAF and USAF planes over the no-fly zones; he profited from the Oil-for-Food scandal while Iraqi children starved to death; he paid $25,000 to the families of each Palestinian suicide-murderer; he threatened his peaceful pro-Western Arab neighbors; he summarily expelled UN weapons inspectors in 1998; and the Iraqi Intelligence Service attempted to assassinate President George Bush senior and the emir of Kuwait with a powerful car bomb in 1993. Furthermore, Iraq sheltered the Mujahedin-e-Khalq Organization (which had killed U.S. soldiers and civilians), the Palestine Liberation Front, Abu Abbas (who murdered the U.S. citizen Leon Klinghoffer on the cruise ship *Achille Lauro*), the Abu Nidal organization (responsible for the deaths or wounding of nine hundred people in twenty countries), Abdul Rahman Yasin (who mixed the chemicals for the 1993 World Trade Center bombing), and several others. Nor did the future look bright post-Saddam; he had two vicious, sadistic, sons, one of whom—Uday—was a rapist and mass murderer.

Yet due to the incessant, strident, and often unjustified criticism from the left-liberal media, today only some 20 percent of the English-speaking peoples support their governments' actions in Iraq and Afghanistan. (One wonders who these fabulously stalwart one-in-five actually are who are so impervious to the endless left-liberal bias? Perhaps there is a sturdy irreducible minimum number of people who believe in attacking enemies rather than appeasing them, whomsoever those enemies may be, come what may? If so, the future hope of the English-speaking peoples lies with them, *American Spectator* readers to the forefront one imagines.)

It is in the off-mainstream media, especially blogs—and of course on Fox News—that one hears of the many and multifarious victories that go virtually unreported elsewhere, but which in earlier wars would have been trumpeted to the skies. A skirmish between British paratroopers and the Taliban in Helmand province in Afghanistan in September 2006 that left nearly 200 Taliban fighters dead at the cost of two Britons wounded, was reported in a British newspaper under the headline "Two Paras Wounded in Clash With Resurgent Taliban." Nor is that an isolated incident of media bias. Neither Lloyd George nor Wilson nor Churchill nor Roosevelt could have won a war faced with that species of headline-writing. It seems to be politically incorrect to record the large numbers of enemy fighters who tend to die when they tangle with our forces in Helmand, whereas the death of a single British infantry soldier there makes the front page of national newspapers here. The numbers of enemy fighters killed—often ten times our troops' numbers or (as in the above case) sometimes many more—are virtually never reported to the English-speaking peoples, who thus understandably feel themselves starved of good news.

SOME OF THE CONTRADICTIONS of the left-liberal approach have gone all but unnoticed by their opponents on the right, with very unfortunate consequences. The BBC criticism of the death penalty imposed on Saddam sat ill with their arguments that Iraq needed to have full political sovereignty; the mantra that many more troops should have been sent to Iraq in 2003 contradicts contemporaneous complaints about "a heavy boot-print on the ground"; the left-liberal glorification of Colin Powell (in order to compare him favorably with Donald Rumsfeld) clashes with the fact that it was he who produced the vial of white powder at the United Nations Security Council to illustrate WMDs; their criticism of de-Ba'athification contradicts their demands at the time for complete and immediate de-Ba'athification; their claims that the Coalition Authority should have kept the Iraqi army intact contradicts their contemporaneous reports that it had disappeared back to its villages; furthermore, do they really think power should have been handed over more quickly by the Garner and Bremer pro-consular authorities to Iraqis (such as Ahmed Chalabi) whom they later denounced as corrupt? Above all, their complaint about the squabbling and in-fighting of the Iraqi parliament completely contradicts their statements that the war was fought for oil, or contracts, or revenge, or imperialism, or anything rather than to impose democracy and destroy a foul dictatorship. Democracy engenders debate (i.e., arguments).

The wars of the English-speaking peoples almost always start out badly, but that should not invalidate them. Today, the rest of the English-speaking peoples have a right to expect leadership from the United States in this great struggle against a bitter, murderous, unappeasable foe of truly dreadful and evil intent. Yet in their midterm elections, Americans effectively cashiered their commander-in-chief after no major defeats on the ground and plenty of (under-reported) victories.

Of course, the 2006 midterms saw a smaller swing against a second-term president than were registered against either Eisenhower or Nixon, yet what solace the hard-pressed but PR-savvy

Taliban, Ba'athist, Hamas, Fatah, Hizbollah, and al Qaeda fighters must have taken from the President's loss of both the House and the Senate. The message it sends is obvious; continue this struggle for a little time longer and the Great Satan will withdraw first from Iraq, then Afghanistan, then from the rest of the Middle East, allowing you to massacre its clients and erect a Caliphate, prior to establishing a great nuclear reckoning with it one day in the future. It might not be an accurate prediction of future events, but that is immaterial since it is undoubtedly the encouragement they have gleaned from the pro-withdrawal stances of people like House Speaker Nancy Pelosi.

For all the criticisms of the Bush administration, and some of the most damaging have also come from Republicans such as Senator John McCain, it ought to be recalled that in no major war of the English-speaking peoples—by which I exclude operations such as the liberation of Grenada in 1983—has everything gone well right from the start. Taken chronologically, a pattern emerges about the way we as a political culture go about the business of warfare that says much about our morality, decency, democracy, and essentially non-militaristic way of life. It is only later on in conflicts that a bitter ruthlessness enters our souls, which is a pre-condition to victory.

If we truly wish for victory in the War on Terror—which it seems only that splendid 20 percent of us really do—it will need to be fought in an altogether tougher way, one from which the liberal consciences of people like Nancy Pelosi shrink. Yet the alternative, of course, is successive humiliations, retreats, and surrenders at the hands of Islamist Fundamentalist Totalitarian Fascism, which we must surmise from the opinion polls is possibly now the American public's preferred route. Having seen what the Khmer Rouge did to ordinary Cambodians after the Americans withdrew from Indo-China in 1975, is the United States seriously proposing to leave millions of Iraqi democrats to the mercy of the jihadists?

UNLIKE IN MANY EARLIER CONFLICTS, there will be no way to tell when al Qaeda and its successors really ever accept defeat in the

War on Terror. The only criterion worth considering will be whether coordinated acts of Islamofascist terror continue to be carried out against the English-speaking peoples. In a world in which weapons are likely to become ever more lethal, hard to detect, and easy to deliver, we must consider a world in our children and grandchildren's time in which large parts of central London, New York, Sydney, and Chicago are rendered uninhabitable for decades as a result of make-shift "dirty" nuclear bombs, with unimaginable social and economic consequences. Such is the true "option of defeat."

Fortunately, as Theodore Roosevelt told Rudyard Kipling, the constituent parts of the English-speaking peoples "are naturally closer than those of any others." With Europe turning towards full-scale appeasement, in them lies the only true prospect for victory.

(September 2007)

Contributors

Fouad Ajami is the Majid Khadduri Professor of Middle East Studies and Director of the Middle East Studies Program at the Paul H. Nitze School of Advanced International Studies of Johns Hopkins University. He is the author of many articles and books on the Middle East, and contributes regularly to journals and periodicals, including (in addition to *The American Spectator*) the *Wall Street Journal, Foreign Affairs*, and *The New Republic*. His most recent book is *The Foreigner's Gift: The Americans, The Arabs, and the Iraqis in Iraq*. In 2006, he received the Bradley Prize for Outstanding Achievement and the National Humanities Medal.

Rod Dermer serves as Israel's Minister of Economic Affairs at the Israeli Embassy in Washington. He was previously a columnist for the *Jerusalem Post*. He is co-author (with Natan Sharansky) of the best-selling book *The Case for Democracy: The Power of Freedom to Overcome Tyranny and Terror* (2004).

Victor Davis Hanson is a Senior Fellow at the Hoover Institution, professor emeritus at California University, Fresno, and a nation-

189

ally syndicated columnist for Tribune Media Services. He is also the Wayne & Marcia Buske Distinguished Fellow in History, Hillsdale College, where each fall he teaches courses in military history and classical culture. His most recent book is *A War Like No Other: How the Athenians and Spartans Fought the Peloponnesian War* (Random House).

Lawrence E. Harrison is a senior research fellow and adjunct lecturer at the Fletcher School, Tufts University. He is the author of numerous articles and several books, most recently of *The Central Liberal Truth* (Oxford University Press, 2006), and co-editor, with Samuel Huntington, of *Culture Matters: How Values Shape Human Progress* (Basic Books, 2000).

Daniel Johnson is a London-based editor and author. He has contributed articles to *Commentary, The New Criterion*, the *New York Sun*, and other leading publications (including *The American Spectato*r). He is currently the editor of *Standpoint*, a new cultural magazine published in London. He is also the author of the recently published *White King and Red Queen: How the Cold War Was Fought on the Chessboard* (Atlantic Books, 2007)).

James Kurth is the Claude Smith Professor of Political Science at Swarthmore College where he teaches courses in defense policy, foreign policy, and international politics. He is the editor of *Orbis* and a senior fellow at the Foreign Policy Research Institute in Philadelphia. He is the author of numerous articles on foreign affairs and international politics that have appeared in such publications as *National Review, The National Interest*, and *Foreign Policy*.

Michael Novak is the George Frederick Jewett Scholar in Religion, Philosophy, and Public Policy at the American Enterprise Institute. He is the author of numerous articles and books, including (most recently) *No One Sees God: The Dark Night of Atheists and Believers,* *Washington's God: Religion, Liberty, and the Father of Our Country* (with Jana Novak, 2006), *The Universal Hunger for Liberty: Why the Clash of Civilizations is Not Inevitable* (2004), and *On Two Wings: Humble Faith and Common Sense at the American Founding* (2001). He is also the author of the widely influential book *The Spirit of Democratic Capitalism* (1982).

James Piereson is President of the William E. Simon Foundation and senior fellow at the Manhattan Institute, where he directs the Center for the American University. He has contributed articles on public affairs to numerous publications, including *Commentary, The Weekly Standard, The New Criterion*, and *The Wall Street Journal*. He is the author most recently of *Camelot and the Cultural Revolution: How the Assassination of John F. Kennedy Shattered American Liberalism* (Encounter Books, 2007).

Norman Podhoretz is the editor-at-large of *Commentary* and the author of ten books, including, most recently, *The Norman Podhoretz Reader* (The Free Press) and *World War IV: The Long Struggle Against Islamofascism* (Doubleday, 2007). In June 2004, Mr. Podhoretz was awarded the Presidential Medal of Freedom, the nation's highest civilian honor.

Andrew Roberts is a London-based writer and the author of numerous books of biography and history. His most recent book is *A History of the English-Speaking Peoples Since 1900* (HarperCollins). Previous works include *Eminent Churchillians* (1994), *Salisbury: Victorian Titan* (1999), and *Hitler and Churchill: Secrets of Leadership* (2003).

Natan Sharansky is a former political prisoner who spent nine years in prison camps in the Soviet Union for his work on behalf of human rights. He has served in various ministerial capacities in four Israeli governments, including Deputy Prime Minister. He is currently the chairman of the Institute for Strategic Studies at the Shalem Center in Jerusalem. In 2004, he co-authored (with Rod Dermer) the best-selling book *The Case for Democracy: The Power of Freedom to Overcome Tyranny and Terror.*

James Q. Wilson is the Ronald Reagan Professor of Public Policy at Pepperdine University. He has previously been Professor of Government at Harvard University and of Public Policy at UCLA. His books include *Thinking about Crime, Crime and Human Nature* (with Richard J. Herrnstein), and *On Character.* He is a past president of the American Political Science Association. In 2003, he received the Presidential Medal of Freedom, the nation's highest civilian award.

Index

Augustus, 156

Australia, capitalism in, 54; democracy in, 15; military of, 180–182; representation in, 4

Austria, democracy in, 18, 20, 22; representation in, 4

Aylwin, Patricio, 61

Baath Party, 110, 146, 157, 167, 187; de-Baathification, 186

Bachelet, Michelle, 61

Badawi, Zaki, 86–87

Baker, James, 97–98, 102, 161

Balaguer, Joaquín, 60

Bangladesh, Muslims in, 116

Barbary Pirates, 121

Bawer, Bruce, *While Europe Slept*, 119

Bayles, Martha, 15–16

BBC, 8, 114, 182, 186

Benedict XVI, 85–86

Benda, Julien, 84

Berlinski, Claire, *Menace in Europe*, 119

Biden, Joseph, 105

Bill of Rights, 11

Bipartisan Campaign Reform Act (McCain-Feingold), 5

Blair, Tony, 81, 83, 88, 178–179, 181

Blankley, Tony, *The West's Last Chance*, 119

Blix, Hans, 124

Boer War, 178

Bolivia, democracy in, 31, 62–63

Borah, William, 102

Bosch, Juan, 59–60

Bosnia, 87, 157

Brandeis, Louis, 6

Brazil, democracy in, 31, 61

Bremer, Paul, 186

British West Indies Regiment, 181

Brooks, Arthur, *Who Really Cares*, 10

Buchanan, Patrick J., 36

Buckley, William F., Jr., 36

Bulgaria, democracy in, 33

Bush, George, 98, 161, 184

Bush, George W., administration, 29, 92–93, 154, 187; and Blair, 178; democratization projects of, 19,

21–22, 56–57, 102–106, 119, 122–125, 138–139, 141, 143, 147–150; Doctrine, 21, 36, 42–46, 48, 50–51; First Inaugural Address, 131–132; Second Inaugural Address, viii–ix, 1, 21, 35–52, 90, 109, 120–121, 132–133, 144, 175; speeches, 89, 104, 124–125, 170; and the war in Iraq, x, 81, 88, 96–97, 162, 167, 176, 179–188

Caesar, 156

Cambodia, 157, 187; democratization projects in, 20

Canada, democracy in, 15; democracy promotion of, 64; Loyalists in, 14; military of, 180–181; Quebec, 69–70; representation in, 4; welfare in, 14

Carothers, Thomas, 118

Carter, Jimmy, 61, 167

Castro, Fidel, 134

CBS, 182

Chalabi, Ahmed, 186

Chamorro, Violeta de, 61

Channel Four (UK), "Dispatches," 85

Charles the Hammer (Charles Martel), 128

Chávez, Hugo, 61, 118

Chechnya, 87

Chen Shuibian, 68

Chesterton, G. K., *Lepanto*, 75–76

Chiang Ching-Kuo, 68

Chiang Kai-Shek, 68

Chicago Times, 37, 39

Chile, Basques in, 70; entrepreneurship in, 69–71; democracy in, 31, 61–62

China, democratization in, 32–33, 68–69, 175; government of, 47; military of, 157; as threat, 67, 119; Tiananmen Square demonstration, 144

Chirac, Jacques, 88

Chomsky, Noam, 84

Churchill, Winston, 174, 178, 185

CIA, 59

Cicero, 156

Clinton, Bill, 97, 124, 167; administration, 154, 168

Syrian Protestant College (American University of Beirut), 103

Tablighi Jamaat, 86
Taft, William Howard, 18, 58
Taheri, Amir, 50
Taiwan, democracy in, 19, 32, 57, 66–69
Taliban, 106, 132, 167, 183, 185, 187
Thailand, free markets in, 55
Thatcher, Margaret, 7, 178
Thebes, 160
Thucydides, 160
Tiger, Colonel Blair, 78–79
Tocqueville, Alexis de, *Democracy in America*, 3, 8–10, 55, 63, 111, 114
Trainor, Bernard, 162
Transparency International, Corruption Perceptions Index, 71
Trujillo, Rafael Leonidas, 59
Truman, Harry S, Inaugural Address, 40–42, 46–48, 175; Truman Doctrine, 41, 48
Tufts University, Fletcher School, 66
Turkey, democracy in, 2, 15, 23, 40–41, 46, 56, 169; and the Kurds, 24, 148; military in, 159; Ottoman Empire, 27–28, 76–77, 92, 102–104

Ukraine, democracy in, 2, 33, 51, 144
United Nations, in the Balkans, 168; Development Program, 64; resolutions, 145, 184; Security Council, 186; surveys, 62; Universal Declaration of Human Rights, 54; weapons inspectors from, 124, 184
United States, Alliance for Progress, 60–62; and Britain, 178–188; Civil War, 5, 75, 182; Constitution, 3–5, 12–13, 45; crime rates in, 7; Department of Defense, 64; Electoral College, 2; federalism in, 5–8; Founding Fathers of, 85; freedom in, 11–14; Government Accountability Office, 62–63; as Great Satan, 142, 187; high culture of, 15–16; immigrants to, 70; lawyers in, 11–12; polls of,

2–3; popular culture of, 15–16; religion in, 9–11; representation in, 4; Revolutionary War, 12, 173, 177; social programs and welfare in, 4, 14; USAID, 62–66; terrorism in, 135
Uruguay, democracy in, 31, 62
USS *Cole*, 170
USS *New York*, 79

Venezuela, democracy in, 2, 31, 61–62, 118
Vidal, Gore, 84
Vietnam, War, ix, 77, 154, 158, 162, 178, 182–183
Voice of America, 144

Walker, Edwin, 154
Wall Street Journal, The, 39
War on Terror, 174, 179–180
Washington, George, 177; Farewell Address, 121
Washington Consensus, 31, 55, 69
Washington Post, 182
Weather Underground, 10
Weiler, Joseph, 76
Welles, Sumner, 58–59
West Point, 78–79
Wilhelm, 77
Will, George, 36
Wilson, James Q., 174–175
Wilson, Woodrow, vii; democratization projects of, 17–19, 58, 102–103, 175; Inaugural Address, 41–41; in wartime, 185
Wilsonianism, 19–20, 102–104, 178
Winik, Jay, *April 1865*, 181
Woodward, Bob, 162
World Bank, 54–55, 64
World Trade Center, 79; 1993 bombing, 185
World War I, 5, 17, 78, 162, 179–181; casualties during, 183
World War II, 15–16, 23–24, 42, 48, 77, 161–162, 179–181; alliances during, 150, 174; casualties during, 183